SHOPLIFTERS vs. RETAILERS
The Rights of Both

Charles A. Sennewald, CMC, CPP

my regards to Evangeline Pappas!
Chuck Sennewald
June 19, 2000

SHOPLIFTERS vs. RETAILERS
The Rights of Both

Charles A. Sennewald, CMC, CPP

Disclaimer
   The scenarios contained herein closely resemble actual cases. However, the names of retailers and their employees, as well as the customers have been changed to protect the privacy of the participants. Further, my analysis of the various scenarios is but this author's opinion based on years of experience and should not be construed as legal advice.

Library of Congress Cataloging-in-Publication Data

Sennewald, Charles A.
    Shoplifters vs. Retailers
    The Rights of Both

    p.   cm.

ISBN 1-890035-18-1
Library of Congress Card Number: 00-101429

New Century Press
1055 Bay Boulevard, Suite C
Chula Vista, California 91911
(619) 476-7400
(800) 519-2465

Cover design by New Century Press

10 9 8 7 6 5 4 3 2 1

Printed in the United States of America

Foreword

It has been my pleasure to know Chuck Sennewald as a fellow-professional, a scholar, an unparalleled security expert in the field ...and as a friend. The respect and reputation he enjoys in the security industry is second to none. It is only understandable that such a man would discover the need for an excellent document such as you soon will be reading between these covers. Shoplifting is a silent killer to the economy of this great country by causing retailers to lose billions to these criminal efforts. It also ruins the lives of thousands and thousands of persons by giving them a criminal record.

Sennewald's latest writing effort is one that has filled a genuine need for both the retailer and shoplifter, to better understand the consequences to both parties from this pernicious crime. It is a book that needs to be on the shelves or in the libraries of retailers, lawyers, security managers and anyone involved in the protection of assets of retail stores. I know the book will be a valued help to all who work in these fields.

Clifford E. Simonsen, Ph.D., CPP
Camano Island, WA
January 2000

Preface

In early 1999 this author constructed a website www.shoplifting.com which spelled out, among other things, the recommended "six steps" security agents should follow prior to detaining a person engaged in or suspected of shoplifting. The site was conceived as a resource for security personnel who require more information about and a better understanding of their responsibilities. The site invited questions with the promise of a response.

Surprisingly, only a very few security practitioners posed any questions. Rather, a constant stream of questions were asked by persons who themselves had been stopped, detained or arrested for shoplifting, or from persons who purportedly were relatives or "friends" of persons so detained. Some questions, framed as a narrative of what had occurred, concluded with questions such as, "...because this is my first time do you think I will have to go to jail?"...or "I've received a letter from the store demanding $200.00. What right do they have to bill me and must I pay?"... or "What authority did they have to hold me in handcuffs?" Some questions were humorous; some pathetic, others cried for help and information. It became abundantly clear that those caught up in this mischief, this crime commonly called "shoplifting," really had nowhere to go to get answers. They felt they couldn't ask the store that arrested them, nor did they feel they could get answers from the police who processed them. Wasn't there some other source of information rather than an attorney-at-law?

At the same time it became clear that despite all the progress that has been made in the retail sales industry to upgrade and professionalize its security programs, too many security employees still either ignore the rules or take chances, that, although well-intended, result in pain, injury, and/or embarrassment to themselves and the public and result in legal risk and exposure to their employer.

This booklet is a serious attempt to help both the retailer and the shoplifter to understand and clarify many issues that affect both sides of this on-going problem of shoplifting.

Acknowledgements

This work is the consequence of those many questions sent to my website ...wherein it became clear that there were too many people being arrested for shoplifting who didn't have a clue as to what the process was all about. It also became apparent to me that many retail security practitioners, interestingly, lacked insight into this retail theft area, commonly referred to as "shoplifting."

I shared the concept of this project with my colleagues and fellow-members of the International Association of Professional Security Consultants (IAPSC) and was delighted that a good number of them volunteered many helpful suggestions and much encouragement. For all of that, from fellow-professionals, I'm thankful and grateful. Several colleagues took the time to read drafts and offered professional criticism and advice, including: John Case, CPP, Jerry O'Rourke, CPP, Roger Griffin, CPP, Michael Magill, and Don Wagner. To all of them I extend my gratitude. To my good friend and fellow- IAPSC and India Club co-member, Cliff Simonsen, Ph.D., CPP, I am especially grateful and hereby acknowledge his particularly valuable advice regarding the format and his time and talent in reviewing and copyediting this work. Lastly, to those gentlemen who were willing to review the draft and go "on the record", as reflected on the back cover of this book, I'm particularly grateful! Who would we be and where would we be without such friends?

Dedication

I dedicate this work to:
My wonderful wife Connie ("Precious");
to our grandchildren, with the prayer they will
always see and understand the difference
between right and wrong;
and to the Holy Spirit.

TABLE OF CONTENTS

FOREWORD v

PREFACE. vii

ACKNOWLEDGEMENTS ix

DEDICATION xi

INTRODUCTION 1

THE OBJECTIVES OF THIS BOOKLET. 3

SHOPLIFTING DEFINED 4

TYPICAL SHOPLIFTING ACTS 4

IS SHOPLIFTING A MISDEMEANOR OR A
FELONY?. 5

WHAT ARE THE DIFFERENCES AMONG A
STOP, DETENTION AND ARREST? 5

WHAT IS "CIVIL RECOVERY"? 6

THE "SIX STEP RULE" USED BY RETAILERS 7

WHO HAS THE AUTHORITY TO DETAIN OR
ARREST? 8

CAN STORE PERSONNEL USE FORCE TO
BRING A PERSON BACK TO THE STORE? 9

ONCE YOU'RE IN CUSTODY AS A JUVENILE. 9

ONCE YOU'RE IN CUSTODY AS AN ADULT 9

IS THE STORE REQUIRED TO ADVISE A
SUSPECTED SHOPLIFTER OF HIS/HER
RIGHTS? 10

WHAT DOES BEING "TRESPASSED" MEAN? 11

WHAT HAPPENS IF AN ACCUSED PLEADS
"GUILTY"? 12

WHAT HAPPENS IF AN ACCUSED PLEADS
"NOT GUILTY"? 12

CATEGORIES OF SHOPLIFTING INCIDENTS 13

"STOPS" AND "NON-PRODUCTIVE STOPS" 14

KNOWLEDGE OF OTHERS ENGAGED IN
THEFT AND PURSUITS 28

DETENTION AND ARREST 37

THREATS AND PROMISES. 45

USE OF HANDCUFFS AND USE OF FORCE 51

FITTING ROOMS AND SEARCHES 58

EAS (ELECTRONIC ARTICLE SURVEILLANCE
SYSTEMS) & SEARCHES 69

MERCHANDISE DISPLAYED BEYOND THE
REGISTERS 81

ARMED SECURITY 91

BASIC SECURITY DO'S AND DON'TS. 92

THE GRAND DILEMMA. 94

ABOUT THE AUTHOR 97

Introduction

Every day approximately 5,400[1] persons are detained and /or arrested in the United States for the crime of shoplifting, and this happens <u>every single day</u>! Retail security experts have ventured the estimate that for each person caught in the act, as many as <u>35</u> acts of shoplifting go undetected. Run those numbers and you come up with 69,000,000 acts of shoplifting each year. Is it any wonder that current data indicate the annual loss caused by shoplifting amounts to <u>$16 billion</u>![2] So, to the retailer, this is serious business. And, for each of the many thousands caught each day, this becomes a serious life event. Both sides have their rights, however, and are adamant about ensuring their rights are protected and respected.

Your author has written this helpful booklet in order to try to clarify the rights of persons caught and accused of shoplifting and inform the shopping public as to the retailer's rights to deal with shoplifting and the actions of security agents. Nowhere else is this kind of information available in a single resource document. In addition to spelling out the rights of both parties involved in a shoplifting incident, this work should provide some enlightenment to those who believe they've been wronged under civil law.

---

1. *Shoplifters Alternative*, Jericho, NY
2. National Retail Federation, 1988

It is hoped this knowledge will help discourage and reduce the number of frivolous lawsuits. On the other hand, if the accused was not properly dealt with, this knowledge may provide some basis for possible recourse. It's not the intention of this author to play "advocate" for either side, but rather to objectively address a dynamic social and security phenomenon, one which has plagued the retail industry for decades and has brought significant pain, embarrassment and confusion to millions of Americans.

Objectives of This Book

Your author sincerely hopes by writing this book-let to accomplish the following goals:

- Educate the public in regard to the merchant's rights to protect against shoplifting;
- Reiterate to the retail industry the customer's rights;
- Inform the accused of the process they will undergo, once arrested;
- Provide the retailer with a tool to test, or template against which to compare their shoplifting policies and procedures; and
- Provide insight into the practical aspects of shoplifting for the legal community that may be used to differentiate between meritorious and unmeritorious actions.

The reader will find definitions of terms and answers to frequently asked questions by the person accused, and by family members, security practitioners and students alike.

Contained in this booklet are twenty shoplifting scenarios, followed by an analysis of the ramifications of the incident described. You will be taken through the events that lead to a problem with or confrontation between the customer and store security, followed by your author's assessment and examination of this traumatic experience.

Lastly, this work identifies the things that a retailer should and should not do in handling persons suspected of shoplifting..

"Shoplifting" Defined

"Shoplifting" is the common term used to describe that act of theft, which occurs when a customer (or person who appears to be a customer) steals merchandise from a retailer while the store is open to the public. Every state in the union has its own laws that address such crime and more often than not it's statutorily defined as theft, not "shoplifting." Some states have adopted a "common" statute but each state typically deals differently with shoplifting.

Typical "Shoplifting" Acts

The most common types of shoplifting acts include, but are not limited to:

1. Secreting and/or hiding unpaid-for merchandise on one's person or in one's handbag, store bag or other container carried by the offender.

2. Wearing unpaid-for merchandise out of the store.

3. Openly carrying unpaid-for merchandise out of the store.

4. Switching the price tags and paying a lesser price for an item.

5. Exchanging the contents of a package for merchandise of a higher value (for example putting Nikes in a box of cheaper athletic shoes).

6. Selecting an item of merchandise from its display and presenting it for an exchange or refund.

Is Shoplifting a Misdemeanor or a Felony?

Remember, shoplifting is no more or less than an act of theft. The value of the item/s taken usually determines the seriousness of the charge. Each state has a different threshold of price and value that will separate a misdemeanor from a felony. In some states the crime of theft is a misdemeanor if the value of the item taken does not exceed $400.00. In other states that threshold may be lower or higher.

There are some exceptions to this simplistic, but common, distinction. For example, if it can be proven a shoplifter entered the store with the specific intent to commit theft, the conduct could be viewed as a burglary, which is a felony. That specific intent could be established if a shoplifter entered with an empty box and then filled that box with stolen items, or if a shoplifter wore a coat that had been modified and fitted with very large pockets in the lining to accommodate stolen items.

What Are the Differences among a Stop, a Detention and an Arrest?

A "stop" is when a customer's progress is impeded or interrupted by a store employee who essentially is questioning that customer about a transaction or about merchandise. A "stop" is most typically a brief inquiry, seeking a plausible or satisfactory explanation for or about a transaction involving merchandise, and is not intended as accusatory in nature.

A "<u>detention</u>" is the forced (or perceived forced) custody of a person, and should only be done based on "<u>probable cause</u>," and the duration of which is used only to investigate the circumstances of an event. This is only used to determine if the customer, in fact, does have the store's merchandise or not. If the investigation establishes probable cause that the customer is in the process of stealing merchandise, the detention may or may not lead to a complaint to the police and formal <u>arrest</u>. A detention may disclose that the person being detained committed no crime and such person should be immediately released. An individual, during detention, may admit criminal conduct and yet be released without arrest. The use of nondeadly reasonable force and the use of handcuffs may be used in a detention.

An "<u>arrest</u>" is usually that official act, often required by the police, wherein the shoplifter is notified they are "<u>under arrest</u>" and the matter of their criminal conduct is transferred from the private affair of the store to be handled now by the criminal justice system.

What Is "Civil Recovery?"

Most states have enacted laws that allow the merchant to recover some of the costs incurred to deal with the problem of shoplifting. As an example, the store must incur the expense of hiring security employees to detect and apprehend shoplifters...a significant expense. If the criminal court fines the shoplifter, the money collected then goes to the local or state government... <u>not</u> to the store. "Civil recovery" is a "fine" that goes to the store to help offset their losses and security expenses. The demand is usually made by the store in the form of a letter, sent within weeks after the arrest, with the amount specified. If the shoplifter ignores or refuses to pay that demand (which could amount to as much as $500.00), the store can take the offender into civil court. A shoplifter need not be arrested and turned over to the police to receive this civil demand. The demand can be triggered just by a detention.

The "Six Step Rule" Used by Retailers

Many retail security practitioners are trained to follow the "six step rule" before making a stop or detention. The use of the word "rule" is self-imposed and internalized, meaning it's not a state law that mandates the six step rule. The corpus delecti (literally "the body of the crime") is what constitutes the necessary elements and facts for a lawful arrest.

An agent can break the "rule" and still have a valid and lawful arrest for theft. The "six step rule" is only meant as a guideline for agents, and adherence to such guidelines tends to protect the public from being falsely accused of theft and at the same time tends to protect the agent and retailer from making serious mistakes. Those six steps are:

1. The agent should see the subject approach the merchandise.
2. The agent should personally see the subject take physical possession of the merchandise.

3. The agent should personally see <u>where the merchandise is</u> concealed.
4. There should always be maintained <u>uninterrupted surveillance</u> of the subject, once they have taken possession. (A momentary loss of view because another customer passes between or the subject walks past a pillar doesn't necessarily constitute an interruption.)
5. The agent should see that the <u>subject does not pay for the goods</u>.
6. The agent should make the <u>stop after the subject leaves the store</u> because it only goes that much further to establish the person had no intention of paying for the item/s.

It only makes sense that if indeed a security agent meticulously follows such rules, the chance for an error to occur would be very remote.

Who Has the Authority to Arrest or Detain?

The <u>only</u> person who can make an <u>arrest</u> for <u>shoplifting is the person who witnesses the act</u>. That's to say, a store employee who believes someone stole an item (but didn't see it happen) can't arrest that person based on suspicion, nor can the police arrest a misdemeanant based on suspicion.

On the other hand, most states have either codified or case law which allows a merchant to temporarily and reasonably <u>detain</u> a customer if there is reasonable and probable cause to believe a theft has occurred, and to conduct a reasonable investigation in a reasonable period of time to recover their merchandise.

Can Store Personnel Use Force in Bringing a Person Back to the Store?

Typically, state law allows the merchant or his/her agent the right to use a "reasonable" amount of non-deadly force to detain and overcome resistance and return the suspected shoplifter to the store, so that an investigation can be conducted. If the state did not allow the merchant or his agent to use some force (including the use of handcuffs) the customer could simply walk away and, if he or she did steal, take the merchandise with them.

Once You Are in Custody as a Juvenile

The retailer has two viable options when detaining a juvenile: Either they turn the youngster over to the police or call the parents and require them (or some other adult, such as a custodian) to come and take custody of the young offender. When the adult arrives, the security employee or store representative will explain what occurred. The police could refer the matter to juvenile authorities or the juvenile court for their administrative processing of the offender or simply take the child home to the parents. In all likelihood, the parents will receive a demand for "civil recovery" subsequent to this event.

Once You Are in Custody as an Adult

Typically, store personnel initially detain an adult customer. This detention is a status that terminates either in a suspect's release, with or without an admission of guilt or, it can result in being formally arrested. An arrest is necessary if the matter is being referred to the criminal justice system. The police report memorializes the event and is used to refer the case to the Prosecutor's office. The Prosecutor, City Attorney, County Attorney or a District Attorney, typically issues a criminal complaint alleging theft, and the matter is referred to the court.

The arrested party, now known as the "Defendant", appears before the court at the appointed time, is advised of the charges and is asked to enter a plea to such charge. An accused may appear with or without an attorney. The entering of a plea is the simple process of standing before the court and answering, "Guilty" or "Not Guilty." An accused may also ask the court for some time before entering a plea, called a "continuance." If granted the court will set a new date for an accused to appear again.

Is the Store Required to Advise Suspected Shoplifters of Their Rights?

No. The advising of rights (the reading of the Miranda Warning), such as the right to remain silent and the right to have an attorney, is required of those who represent the government, the police or other governmental law enforcement officials. Retail security agents do not represent the people or any governmental agency, but represent their employer, the victim store, and are exempt from this legal requirement. Therefore, all admissions and other statements made to the security people are admissible as evidence. If the police are summoned to the store and before they question the person being detained for shoplifting, those officers will most likely "Mirandize" the subject. If the subject agrees to an understanding of those rights and is willing to waive those rights, <u>everything</u> they admit to or say to the police can later be offered as evidence in court.

What Does It Mean to be "Trespassed"?

Some stores will "trespass" a person caught shoplifting. Trespassing can be an end in itself or as a part of the whole process, i.e., the person is informed they will not be prosecuted (the police will not be summoned) but they are not allowed to return to the store, or the person will be referred to the criminal justice system as well as instructed not to return to the store.

To be "trespassed" simply means the customer has become a *"persona non grata,"* a person not wanted. More often than not the process of trespassing a customer/shoplifter is recorded on a pre-printed form which the shoplifter is asked to sign. If the person refuses to sign the form, it's marked as "refused to sign" and simply attached to the other report/s that memorialize the incident. Those companies that do "trespass" usually specify the amount of time the person may not return to the store. Should one ignore this warning, the police may be summoned.

What Happens When an Accused Pleads "Guilty?"

The court may ask if an accused is ready for sentencing. If the accused responds "Yes," the judge can then impose the sentence at that time. The sentence is normally predicated on such factors as: 1) Is this a first offense? 2) Was the accused cooperative with or resistive to the store security employees? 3) Was the accused cooperative with the police when they arrived? 4) Was the accused contrite then, and contrite with the court now? Typical sentences for misdemeanor shoplifters are nominal fines (often only $100 to $500), community service, and/or a time of summary probation. Confinement is unusual for first-time offenders who were and now are cooperative. Repeat offenders, of course, are more likely to receive jail time.

What Happens When an Accused Pleads "Not Guilty?"

Pleading "Not Guilty" means the accused disputes the charge and the accused wants a trial, either by a judge (a bench or court trial) or a trial with a jury in which local citizens (your peers) will determine your innocence or guilt.

The judge will undoubtedly want to know if the accused is represented by an attorney and may inquire if the accused has funds to retain counsel. The judge may refer the accused to the public defender's office for representation if the accused cannot afford an attorney. Again, remember, every state and even different jurisdictions within a given state have varying protocols.

Having said all that...and now that the accused has been detained and/or released, arrested, cited or "booked" by the police, the accused may have a number of questions about the shoplifting incident and what the store did to place the accused in the present situation.

Categories and Examples of Shoplifting Incidents

As indicated earlier, "shoplifting" or "suspected shoplifting" incidents usually fall into three categories: (1) <u>Stops</u>, (2) <u>Detentions</u>, and (3) <u>Arrests</u>. So-called "stops" are typically brief in duration and after an exchange of relatively few words, the matter is concluded. Many incidents in which there's a detention or detention followed by an arrest may be similar. But as remarkably similar as they may appear, the smallest nuance can often change the category or status of that incident. Two equally qualified experts may view the same event differently, based on their own interpretation of events and their own experiences.

To better understand the diversity and complexity of shoplifting acts and the problems connected with them, the following scenarios are provided for the reader's information and understanding. There are 20 such scenarios, each followed by your author's analysis.

"Stops" and "Non-Productive Stops"

Scenario 1A: (*Customer's Viewpoint*): Gloria, a local schoolteacher, strolled through the aisles and selected numerous items from the sale racks of a popular discount store. There were lots of customers, and merchandise was scattered everywhere due to the big sale. After she had patiently waited in a long line, her items were duly recorded, or so she thought. She handed the sales clerk her credit card and told her to charge her account. She took her purchases, which had been placed in a large plastic store bag. As she stepped off the curb heading for her car in the parking lot, the sales clerk called out to her, waving her arms as she approached the customer. "I'm sorry," the employee said, somewhat out of breath, "but may I please take a quick look in your bag?" "Why?" Gloria asked the clerk, raising an eyebrow. "I think we failed to ring one of your tops," replied the flustered employee. Gloria relaxed and opened her bag. The clerk looked into the bag and appeared relieved. "My mistake, miss. Sorry for the inconvenience," said the clerk, then quickly turned and dashed back into the store. Gloria stood there, wondering what in the heck that was all about. When she got home she phoned her sister and related the event. Her sister said the store should never have done that.

Scenario 1B: (*Employee's Viewpoint*): Nicole, the cashier at register station # 8, was coming to the end of a hectic shift and had just completed checking out and bagging a customer's purchases. When she looked around the counter, she realized that a red striped blouse that the customer before the departing woman had decided not to purchase, was gone. It had been lying on the edge of the checkout stand, but was now nowhere in sight. She thought, Oh no, I must've accidentally gathered it up with all the other things and included it in the last lady's bag. Spotting the customer going out the door, Nicole ran after her and caught up to her in the roadway. She politely explained that she may have missed ringing up a blouse in the bag and asked if she could look in the bag. The customer was pleasant and allowed her to look. She couldn't miss that red striped blouse...but it just wasn't there. She thanked the customer and quickly returned to the store, confused as to what had happed to the missing garment.

Analysis: *It's not a very common occurrence for employees to make such a request, yet it's not an <u>unreasonable</u> thing to happen. The customer wasn't accused of stealing. The employee indicated an error may have occurred and asked to see the customer's purchases. The customer cooperated and was thanked. Better to have done this right on the spot rather than request the customer return to the store, which would have magnified the event.*

Now...here is an interesting point. "Regular" sales employees have more latitude to challenge or inquire with certain "immunity" than a security employee. There's a presumption that a security employee's challenge is accusatory in nature, whereas a regular employee's job is to care for their merchandise and for their customer. Nicole could have been concerned her customer might be suspected of taking the red striped blouse when she herself may have put it in the customer's bag in error.

ⓒⓒⓒⓒⓒ

Scenario #2A: (*Customer's Viewpoint*): Sadie's heart was always in her throat when she left the store, because she couldn't resist putting one small item into her sack or bag before leaving. It was an awful habit, and she constantly expected to get caught. Today she had taken a 99-cent pincushion and casually dropped it into the bag while pretending to look at another item. "Excuse me," came a voice from behind, and Sadie almost jumped out of her shoes with fright! Oh no. Caught! I've got to get out of this, she thought. "Excuse me, but may I look in your bag?" asked a saleslady, quite timidly. Sensing power because of the timid approach of the store employee, Sadie shouted, in a loud and demanding voice, "Why?" "I think we didn't charge you for an item," responded the employee, apparently now wishing she wasn't involved with this incident. "Didn't charge me for something?" shouted Sadie, "Are you saying I stole something? Are you accusing me of stealing something?" Sadie was startled by her own sense of indignation and no longer was fearful of being caught or even accused. Her adrenaline was pumping. She almost wanted to be forced back into the store because she felt this strong offense was a great defense. A momentary stare-down elapsed and the employee, without another word, returned to the store. Sadie proudly went to her car and headed for home. As she drove along she pulled out the orange-colored pumpkin-shaped pincushion, sighed over the relief of stress and said to herself, All for 99 cents! No more of this. I'm a lucky gal and here's one gal who ain't going to push her luck no more. And I better not go back into that store again. They'll remember me.

Scenario 2B: (*Employee's Viewpoint*): Every once in a while Mildred would see or thought she saw someone stealing small items of merchandise, and it always upset her. "What can we do if we think someone is stealing, Mrs. Vander?" she asked the owner's wife. "Well, we don't want to accuse people. Best thing to remember is this: What would you do if you owned this store instead of Carl Vander? What would you do?" "I guess I'd kind of pretend that maybe a mistake was made and hope they'd give it back or pay for it," responded Mildred. "Yep, and also provide good customer service. Being right there helps prevent people from taking." Only days after that discussion Mildred saw this large, heavy-set woman customer come into the store again, the same customer she had suspected of stealing a package of safety pins a couple weeks back. She watched the woman from behind the rack of ribbons. The woman's movement was fast, but it sure looked like the lady had a pumpkin pincushion in her hand and then it was gone. Bracing herself for a confrontation, she decided to talk to the customer, but before she could get to her, the lady had walked out of the store. Mildred followed her and said, "Excuse me. I need to look in your bag," words which took a lot of courage. To her amazement the customer shouted at her and wanted to know if she was accusing her of stealing. She decided the wisest course of action would be to disengage and retreat, which she did. She then told Mrs. Vander when she came in later that day and they all agreed to watch for this particular customer in the future and stay with her all the time she was in the store. Mildred went home that night with a sense of having done a courageous act and felt good about herself.

Analysis: *Some people out there can psychologically turn the tables on the store employees, sometimes even trained security employees. The customer wasn't accused of stealing. The employee indicated an error may have occurred and asked to see her purchases. This customer chose to refuse to cooperate and started to make a scene. The employee opted to avoid any further contact and left. The employee, who in good faith believes an error may have occurred or even an act of theft may have occurred, has the right to conduct a reasonable inquiry, and she did. She also has the right to exercise good judgment and avoid the possibility of escalating what was beginning to be an unpleasant scene, mistake or no mistake. It so happens in this scenario, the customer did indeed commit an act of theft. What if the customer had not committed such an act? Was the conduct of the employee appropriate? Of course it was! Now the reader shouldn't get the impression that a refusal to cooperate is a smart strategy; more often than not it can backfire. One valuable lesson is this: So one got away! Ever hear of the old adage: "Better safe than sorry?" There are* *times when good judgment dictates what would prove to be the safer course of action.*

☯☯☯☯☯

Scenario 3A: (*Customer's Viewpoint*): Jimmy had no sooner let the door to the store start to swing shut when a young man with a military-style haircut wearing a sweatshirt and jeans appeared on his right side saying, "Excuse me, sir, I'm with the store's Loss Prevention Department. I think you forgot to pay for something. Would you give it to me please?" The man was holding up some kind of identification card with a photo on it. Jimmy didn't really think the man was talking to him, but there he was, looking straight at him. "I'm sorry, you must have the wrong person. I don't have anything I didn't pay for." "What about the item you have in your right rear pocket?" "That's mine, buddy," said Jimmy, trying to look and act normal in view of this unexpected challenge. "You'll have to return inside so we can sort this out. It'll only take a few minutes." The security man, certainly larger and more physically fit than Jimmy, pointed towards the doors. Once inside the security room, with all the TV screens on the back wall flickering, the man took Jimmy's bag, dumped the contents on the desk and then asked him to remove the "wallet" from his right rear pants pocket. Jimmy, remaining silent while his mind raced, pulled the wallet out of his pocket and handed it to the agent. The agent examined the brand-new wallet and then examined the receipt. All five items, including the wallet, were reflected on the receipt. "Where's your regular wallet?" asked the agent. Jimmy then removed his old wallet from his left rear pants pocket. "Why in the world did you put this new wallet in your pocket instead of leaving it in the bag?" "I don't know, I just wanted to see how it felt, I guess." "Well, there's been a mistake and I'm sorry to have inconvenienced you. You're free to go. Oh, here's the factory insert card that fell out of the wallet before you put it in your pocket. Sorry about this."

"Well, how could such a mistake be made?" asked Jimmy, feeling his anger creeping up. "A sales associate said she saw you carrying the wallet in your hand and saw you stick it in your pocket. She apparently thought you hadn't paid for it," he replied. Jimmy walked past the agent and out of the store, angry, and wondering which of the employees had caused this to happen. This unpleasant 10-minute "detour" had seemed like an hour.

Scenario 3B: (*Employee's Viewpoint*): The newest assistant manger in men's furnishings rushed up to Rod, one of the store's Loss Prevention Agents, and excitedly whispered, "See that guy right there?" She pointed to a young customer walking towards the exit doors. "He just took this card out of one of our wallets and stuck the wallet in his right rear pocket...he's shoplifting it right now!" She was excitedly bouncing up and down in her enthusiasm. Rod knew through his training that an agent can't act on someone else's word, but this appeared to be clear-cut. The factory wallet insert was proof. He followed the customer out the doors and followed all proper procedures. The customer looked shocked when confronted, one of the sure signs of guilt, he thought.

That shocked look was transferred to Rod's face when he realized the wallet was one of the items purchased on the kid's receipt. As soon as he realized the error, he apologized and immediately released the customer, knowing time was important. Experts might argue the issue of whether or not Rod had "probable cause" in this case.

Analysis: *This is commonly referred to as a "Non-Productive Stop." The retail industry over the last century has experienced literally millions of such contacts. The test for store liability rests with such factors as the* <u>reasonableness</u> *of the inquiry, the time involved, the courteous conduct of the store employee (or absence thereof) and whether the customer was "injured" as a consequence of the contact. Remember, the retailer has the right to conduct a reasonable investigation based on probable cause. Certainly, the period of time the customer was delayed would not be considered unreasonable. This is a classical mistake in shoplifting detection work... acting on what someone else says happened. Trained retail security agents know better than to stop someone based on someone else's word or observation. Why? This case is a good example. The assistant manger had not seen the entire event. She didn't see the customer purchase the wallet along with other items. She didn't see the customer remove the wallet from the bag and examine it. She only saw a part of what occurred and that alone looked like the customer was stealing. She couldn't say if the fac-*

tory insert was intentionally discarded or dropped accidentally. And either way, that wouldn't make a difference. This employee is not really to blame. She's not required to witness everything a customer does to ensure the whole event is witnessed. It's not her job. And we still would want her to report what she feels is suspicious. The employee's suspicions can be helpful to security personnel, but can't always be the basis for a stop or detention action. For a professional security employee to stop a customer based on another's observation violates a long-standing industry rule and operating practice.

๛๛๛๛๛

Scenario 4A: (*Customer's Viewpoint*): Amy Miller had finished shopping earlier than expected and was pleased with her choice of the baby shower gift and its wrapping. After getting off the escalator she couldn't help but notice the special sales sign at the sunglasses display, so she stopped to see what they had. Her sunglasses were propped up above her forehead in her thick, blond hair. She pulled them off and set them on the glass counter as she removed an attractive pair from the rack and slid them over her eyes.

She peered into the mirror on the rack and thought to herself, Not bad, but I don't think so. She set those glasses on the counter and selected another pair. I hate the way they hang the tag on the nose piece, she mused as a pleasant voice behind her said, "My, those are attractive on you. May I be of assistance?"

"Gee, I don't know. The price is right but honestly I don't think I need another pair." "Well, if you lose sunglasses like I do, an extra pair wouldn't hurt, especially at this price," said the clerk. Amy just smiled, removed those glasses and set them on the counter with the others. The clerk was called away. Amy tried on one more pair, set them down, looked around, then picked up her sunglasses, slid them on, looked at herself in the mirror again. Satisfied she liked hers best, she decided she didn't need another pair despite the good price. She pulled off her glasses, folded them up, and with her right hand stuck them into her tennis jacket pocket.

After exiting from the store, she was approached by a casually dressed woman holding up a metal badge saying, "I'm with store security. Please hand me the sunglasses in your right jacket pocket." Amy, who had stopped dead in her tracks, looked at the woman and said with a hostile tone in her voice, "I beg your pardon?" She was again asked to hand the woman her sunglasses. "I will do no such thing," said Amy. The woman moved closer and with her eyes fixed on Amy said, "This is not the place for us to discuss the glasses. You'll have to return to the store with me and we can talk about it there." "I'm not giving you my glasses and I'm not returning to the store. You're making some kind of big mistake."

"We'll see who's making the mistake," replied the security agent, as she seized Amy's arm and with a strong grip, guided Amy back into the store. Amy, an athletic woman herself, momentarily thought about resisting but decided to allow the woman to force her along, confident she would be in a stronger position, once the matter was resolved. But then she got angry. In the office Amy was confident the store agent was making a mistake but, as the country club's tennis-singles champion and competitive in nature, she thrust the glasses at the agent.

"Are these the glasses you saw me steal?" asked Amy, quite sarcastically. "Yes, ma'am," replied the agent. Once the glasses were in the agent's hand, it was apparent they were not new and obviously not store merchandise. "Well," said the agent, "these are not ours and I owe you an apology. I'm sorry. The way you picked up the glasses and shoved them into your pocket made me think you were taking ours. I'm sorry and you're free to go." "The only place I'm going to now is to your store manager and report you for dragging me back into this store because of your mistake!"

Scenario 4B: (*Employee's Viewpoint*): Connie had just completed the paperwork connected with an arrest for a woman shoplifting sunglasses from the sale display case when she returned to the floor, only to see this blond, her hair heaped on top of her head, dressed in a white tennis outfit pulling glasses from the display rack. Could I be this lucky to have two in a row from the same rack? she thought. From the ladies' handbags section she could watch without being observed. The attractive blond removed her glasses and laid them on the counter. Connie saw the clerk arrive and engage the blond in conversation, while the blond removed another pair from the rack and tried them on. The clerk then left the blonde customer and disappeared behind a pillar. The blond looked around, then with her right hand, picked up from the display case a pair of glasses, tried them on, looked around, then quickly folded them and jammed them into the short-sleeve summer cover-up pocket with her right hand. Number two for the day coming up! thought Connie who then moved even closer. The customer nonchalantly browsed down the counter then made an immediate left and exited the store with Connie close behind.

She moved quickly around the customer's right side and, displaying her security badge and card said, "Excuse me, I'm store security and I'd like to talk to you about the sunglasses in your pocket." The blonde's answer was defiant and impudent. Connie asked for the glasses, but the customer refused to surrender them. Connie said, "This isn't the place to argue. You'll have to return to the store with me." Sensing this lady was not about to return without assistance, she seized her arm and pushed her in the direction of the doors and on through the store to the security office. Once inside, the woman almost hit her with the glasses. Connie's heart sunk. These are dirty and used. God, how could she have switched these on me? I've goofed big time, she thought. She quickly apologized to the customer, who seemed to be gloating over Connie's misery and asked for the store manager.

Analysis: *Now this is yet another "Non-Productive Stop" but one aggravated by the use of some force, and clearly the customer was "detained." The agent* erred. Retail security practitioners who are properly trained know they must observe a customer approach the merchandise to ensure the article in their hand was selected from its display and is not the customer's own property. Clearly, in this scenario, the agent did not follow this requirement. Further, there is no "probable cause" to believe a theft occurred. The agent thought the customer stole merchandise based on incomplete observation, which is carelessness.

It should be noted here that a "detention" connected with a Non-Productive Stop doesn't mean the store incurs liability. The presence of "probable cause" may justify the detention and a minimum amount of force. However, a good case of "probable cause" can fail in justifying a stop, if _excessive_ force is used. The force used in this case wasn't excessive, but was sufficient to justify a complaint.

☯☯☯☯☯

Scenario 5A: (*Customer's Viewpoint*): Kenny and Chub, both 12, came into the store and separated. Chub didn't want Kenny to see or know what he intended doing: He'd come specifically to get the compact flashlight his mother wouldn't buy for him. When he felt it was safe, he tore the light from its cardboard display package and put the small light in his pocket. In the meantime Kenny was over in the book section thumbing through the pages, while he waited for his friend. "Can't find what I'm looking for," said Chub as he came up behind his friend. "Let's go." "Okay," replied Kenny as he set the book down, and the two wound their way out of the store. Once outside two men came up to them and to Kenny's absolute surprise, Chub started running towards G Street. One man took off after Chub and the second man turned towards Kenny, who, frightened by what was going on, decided he better run too and took off in the opposite direction toward H Street. In his flight Kenny tripped on a parking block and fell, skinning his face and elbow. The store employee seized him by the arm and escorted him back to the store and the police were called. On the way back, through his tears, he asked, "Why are you after me? I didn't do nothing." "If you didn't do anything, then why did you run? Well, WHY I asked?" The man stood waiting for an answer. Kenny gulped and shook his head. "I don't know. You guys scared me. Why are you chasing us anyway?"

Back at the store, while they washed his cuts, they determined Kenny hadn't personally taken anything. But he was still reluctant to tell the men Chub's name. When the police arrived, they asked who his friend was and he asked them, "You're not going to call my dad, are you?" He was hoping against hope. The police officer called his home and could tell it was mom on the phone. "Well, ma'am, your boy and his as-yet-unnamed friend were suspected of shoplifting. But, when the store's employees tried to talk to them, they ran like jackrabbits. The other boy got away. We'll... take care of that, but your boy fell down and was caught. He's got some scrapes and cuts, nothing serious. You or your husband need to come down here and pick him up right away." Obviously in response to questions posed by the mother, the officer continued, "No ma'am, apparently it was the other boy who store security observed stealing, but when your boy ran, the store people assumed he'd had taken something too."

Analysis: *This is a classic example of how emotions can interfere with the professional demands of retail security work. Had the second youngster not run, the security personnel probably would not have been interested in him. But the running so strongly suggested complicity, the automatic response kicked-in. Good discipline would have dictated that the focus should have been on the one who did the stealing, not his companion. The running of a small boy, in all likelihood, would probably not rise to the level of "probable cause." Fortunately this child wasn't seriously injured. He may have gotten a tongue-lashing for going with Chub or for running when he didn't have good reason to, depending on the kind of family he comes from. And it may certainly have been an experience Kenny will want to avoid in his future life.*

👀👀👀👀👀

Knowledge of Others Engaged in Theft and Pursuits

Scenario 6A: (*Customer's Viewpoint*): The two boys locked their bikes in the rack and, after a hot dog and soda in the food court, decided to window shop in the mall. "Let's go down and start with the biggest store on the end and work back this way," suggested Mike, the 14-year-old. Obviously they had nothing to waste except time. "Okay," replied Juan, the much larger of the two, although a year younger. In fact, Juan was considered a big boy for his age. The mismatched pair, with pants hanging low and shirts out, made their way into the Anchor Department Store. "Look at this," laughed Juan as he picked up a size small shirt and held it up to his large body. "Just my size." Mike thought his remark was funny too. Juan tossed the shirt back on the pile and the two idly walked among the merchandise, touching many items unnecessarily. It was clearly obvious to customers and clerks alike that these boys weren't seriously shopping. In the center of the store the boys came upon stationery displays and as though looking for trouble, the two scanned the area. "Well, looky-here," said Mike in a toned-down voice, as he pointed to a display fixture of expensive pens sitting on the glass counter. His finger pointed at the fixture door, which was supposed to be locked, but it was slightly ajar. Both boys immediately looked around to see who might have noticed them or their discovery. Seemed like everyone was busy doing their own thing. "Move over this way a little, kind of right here," whispered Mike, motioning with his elbow. Juan obligingly shuffled his large body left, to where Mike indicated. Then ever so gently, Mike partially opened the case door and removed a beautiful blue pen. "$219.95...wow!" gasped Mike as he eyed the price tag. "Whoa!" echoed Juan. Mike knew what he was going to do; Juan did, too, but Juan knew he didn't have the guts to do it. Mike palmed the pen, trying to conceal as much of it as he could, and in an attempt to look "cool" looked slowly in all directions; Juan did, too. Mike pushed the pen into his pocket. "Let's go out into the lot rather than back through the mall," suggested Mike. Juan nodded.

Not 30 feet out of the store the boys heard a male voice call after them, "Hey, you guys...hold up. We want to talk to you." Mike, suspecting the worst, knew he could not get caught again. He darted to his left while, shouting over his shoulder to Juan, "Split man! Go!" Juan, scared to death, lumbered as fast as he could but tripped and fell, the weight of his large body coming down on his wrist causing him awful pain. A young black man grabbed him and started pulling him up. Juan screamed and tears started flowing. "I didn't do anything, I didn't take anything. You can't touch me. Oh, help me! Please just help me!" Paramedics were summoned along with the police. Mike had escaped. Juan admitted he knew what Mike was doing but swore he didn't steal anything, nor had he intentionally helped Mike. He explained his running away for fear of being considered a shoplifter. The officers viewed the videotape and were unsure as to whether Juan knowingly assisted Mike in the theft or not. The parents were advised, and the matter was referred to juvenile authorities for their assessment.

Scenario 6B: (*Employee's Viewpoint*): "Oh-Oh," said Shelley, half to herself. "Here comes trouble." She watched two teenagers on monitor #11 covering men's and boy's clothing. Skip came up and looked over her shoulder. "Could be," he mused. "I'll pull "em up, too," as he sat down and switched from cosmetics over to the camera Shelley was using. "Don't you wonder what their parents are doing or thinking, letting these little stinkers use malls as recreation parks?" "Got nothing better to do, obviously," said Gary, the third security agent on duty at the time. "I'll go down to that area and keep you advised."

"Radio charged?" asked Skip, the senior agent. Gary smiled, "Yep." Both agents followed the boys as they laughed and jostled one another, moving from display to display. "Go home, kids, before you get in trouble," whispered Shelley, as though she was talking to them personally. She often talked to the television screen. There was no sound but she could tell they were engaged in conversation. She wondered what the smaller boy had been saying while pointing. The two boys moved to the stationery counter. Obviously, something had caught their attention. "Have the tape rolling?" asked Shelley. She noted that Skip was now intensely watching the two. "Yeah," he quietly answered, and picked up his radio. "Gary, got "em in view?" "10-4," was the amplified response. As Skip stood up, he keyed his radio, "I'm coming right down. Shelley, stay on top, I have a feeling the fun is turning into serious stuff. I can read their body language. They're going to go for something."

Shelley was now the agent who controlled the detection effort. She observed the big boy maneuvering his body as though attempting to block or cover for his smaller friend. She could still see the smaller boy. "Units 1 and 2, the smaller boy in the black shirt has just removed a pen from the display on the counter," she said on the radio. "It's in his left hand. Okay, he put his left hand into his left front pants pocket. Hand is now out. No pen in sight. The pen's in his left front pants pocket. Do you both read me?" "10-4," she recognized Gary's voice. "10-4," said Skip. I'm not there yet; I'm on the escalator and just now have them in sight. You with them Gary?' "I've got "em in my sights. Keep the camera on "em, Shelley, so he doesn't dump the pen." "10-4," said the woman agent. All could feel the tension building. "They're heading for the east doors," said Shelley. "There they go..." Her voice rose, as she witnessed the two exiting through the right side doors and seconds later saw her two colleagues exiting through the same doors. Shelley could hear the subsequent chase, the sound of running and heavy breathing while the radio mike button was inadvertently held in a transmission mode. The radio static, sounds of muffled shouting, all the excitement and urgency in the request for Shelley to call mall security for help, and the request for paramedics, and the summoning of the police made for an eventful afternoon at the Anchor Department Store.

Analysis: *This is a complicated situation, because different issues have surfaced here. First, security personnel cannot (or should not) detain a person, because such person was aware of another person's crime. Knowing or watching someone else, even a friend or relative, steal, is no crime in itself. On the other hand, if security could prove or establish (e.g., with a video tape) the boy did act as a "lookout" and did position his body to shield the act of theft, that boy would be as guilty of shoplifting as the boy who* pocketed the pen. The breaking of the arm, regrettable as that was, was the consequence of the youngster's attempt to escape, if he was guilty. If the boy didn't assist in the crime but only ran because of fear of what was happening, that injury could be a liability for the store.

Pursuit is another problematical area: Limited pursuits, those limited to the immediate property around the store, which never entail crossing a public street and undertaken in an area where there is little likelihood of innocent bystanders being placed at risk, are usually condoned. Extended pursuits which cross public streets and/or where security employees, suspects or bystanders are at risk, fall below the standard of care in retail security.

❧❧❧❧❧

Scenario #7A: (*Customer's Viewpoint*): It was getting dark, as the two cousins crossed the parking lot of the market. Fritz, the older boy, broke into a jog heading for the doors and Eddie followed. "Let's just look around for bargains," laughed Fritz. Once inside, Eddie wandered into the toy aisle. Fritz went to the cooler area, looking up and down the aisle to see who might be there. I can easily put two cans in my jacket and they'll never know, he thought, as he quickly put a large can of Coors beer in each pocket. "Cool!" he said under his breath. Eddie was still looking at the toy items vacuum-packed in plastic. Fritz sauntered to the candy aisle and again, after checking in both directions and seeing no one, took two candy bars and added them to his "loot" in each pocket. So o o easy, he thought! Not a soul in sight. Fritz headed for the doors, waving Eddie to follow. Eddie, unaware of what Fritz was up to, replaced the package on its hook and started to leave the market. Fritz was already outside and as Eddie approached the door, he saw two tall young men, wearing aprons, reaching for Fritz, who started running, followed by the two men. Eddie, baffled by what he was seeing, started running after the three, and midway in the parking lot caught up with the slower of the two men. As he ran alongside, he asked, "Hey, mister, what's everyone running for?" The agent turned and spoke. "We saw that kid shoplifting and he's trying to get away." The fastest employee caught up with Fritz at the gas station on the corner of the shopping center lot where they stood, when the second employee and Eddie got there. Eddie heard no words exchanged, only saw his cousin handing the beer to the first employee, then saw him drop candy bars on the ground. As the employee started to lean over to pick up the candy, Fritz bolted again. Eddie instantaneously decided to run with his cousin... and the two ran as fast as they could across the street that ran parallel to the freeway, pursued by two store employees. Fritz screamed, "The fence, over the fence!" The two quickly climbed the chain-link fence that enclosed the major freeway and its adjacent property. The fastest employee started to climb and when near the top, froze in his efforts at the sight of the two boys being violently struck by speeding vehicles traveling along the freeway. Both boys were killed.

Scenario 7B: (*Employee's Viewpoint*): It was dinner hour when the store typically wasn't too busy, so Ted, a management employee, was taking advantage of the light traffic to rearrange some shelving. While quietly moving about his work, he observed through the gondola display a teenager who appeared to be nervous and looking up and down the beer display aisle. Oh-Oh! thought Ted. That kid has no business in the liquor area. Bet'cha he's going to try to swipe something. Sure enough, the boy selected two cans of Coors beer, sticking one each in the left and right pockets of his big jacket. Ted noted that the jacket and its pockets were so large the cans didn't even create a bulge. He muttered to himself, There should be a law against big pockets. The boy kind of swaggered away towards the front of the store, turning into the candy aisle. Ted couldn't see clearly but suspected the boy might be swiping candy, too. Ted knew, through store and district management training, the theft had to be observed, but didn't worry about not seeing candy stolen. He already had witnessed the theft of the beer and was satisfied he was going to grab the kid when he left the store.

While keeping his eye on the kid, Larry from the produce department came down the aisle. Ted whispered, "Stay with me, Larry. I'm going after that kid with the red stocking cap. He swiped some beer. We'll get him outside." Larry nodded that he understood and agreed, his heart pounding. He had helped on several shoplifting arrests since starting work at this store, and it was always exciting. Besides, he liked being recognized as an employee that management could always count on if there was something special to do. The minute the boy walked out, the two quickly exited and called after him. The boy turned, looked at them, then broke into a run diagonally across the lot towards the gas station. Ted was gaining on the boy, outrunning his co-worker; but that didn't matter. All he wanted to do was catch this little thief... to teach him a lesson. As the boy's shoes skidded around the back corner of the station, Ted grabbed his flying coat and said, "Ah, I've got'cha. Pull up, pull up." The boy came to a stop. "Gimme those two beers buddy," demanded Ted breathlessly. The shaking boy handed him first one can, then another while saying, "Give me a break, mister. I won't do it again." "I'll bet. Give me the other stuff, too," replied Ted, as he heard Larry arriving.

As the boy was handing over the candy, one bar dropped to the ground. When Ted instinctively stooped to retrieve it, the boy darted off at full speed, followed by a second boy whom Ted had not seen before. "Damnit!" exclaimed Ted...and ran hard after them, wondering why this stranger was now in pursuit, too. Ted's age and his physical fitness were now being challenged. Up ahead the first boy followed by the second, hit the fence and scrambled up it quickly, dropping on the opposite side. When Ted got to that part of the fence, he wearily started to climb it...and watched in horror as the boys ran into the lanes of traffic and were both struck. Bile rose in his throat as he dropped from the fence and vomited. Larry came up gasping for breath and said, "Oh, my God! Oh my God! What's happened here?"

Analysis: *Pursuits must be limited to the property or shopping center in which the store is located. Tragically, too many people have been seriously or fatally injured as a consequence of chasing or being chased to long as a result of shoplifting. An interesting dimension to this particular scenario is the fact the store employees had actually recovered their merchandise, which suggests there should be training to direct employees to consider that fact during a limited pursuit. That is not to say the pursuit should be abandoned, just because the shoplifter throws down the stolen merchandise; that could work in favor of the thief, i.e., steal, if caught, just throw it down and you're home free.*

Too many innocent bystanders have been injured by being bowled over or otherwise knocked to the ground both inside and outside stores during a chase. It would be an unwise policy to totally prohibit security employees the right to engage in a reasonable and limited chase, but great discretion must be exercised along with the limitations already mentioned in this work.

☙☙☙☙☙

Detention and Arrest

Scenario 8A: (*Customer's Viewpoint*): Ms. Jones, a fashionably dressed lady, walked through the door of the Up-Scale Department Store, came to the counter and waited for a clerk...and waited, and waited, repeatedly glancing at her Rolex. She worried about an important appointment she had to keep. Finally, looking around in vain for a sales associate, she walked briskly over to the display counter of scarves, that same one where she had purchased a scarf two days ago to match her favorite sweater. She glanced around impatiently again...trying to find a salesperson in vain. Glancing at her watch again, she decided to simply exchange the scarf, which had been a bad color match. She took the scarf from her purse and placed it on the stack, then quickly selected another, and put in her purse.... and hurried to leave. She looked quizzically as a youthful appearing woman stepped into her path after she exited the store. To her surprise and shock, the agent asked, "Excuse me, I'm with Up-Scale security. I'd like to talk you about the scarf in your purse." This was the start of a long morning for her.

Scenario 8B: (*Employee's Viewpoint*): Betty Johnson, a store Loss Prevention Agent, coming back from a break, noticed as she came through the door a well-dressed woman standing at the cash register who was frequently looking nervously at her watch. After every look at the watch, her eyes swept the area. Betty's pulse quickened...this could be interesting. After a time the woman was observed moving to the display counter of expensive silk scarves, continuing to look around furtively. She then saw the woman take a scarf and stuff it into her purse and hurry out through the south doors. Betty made a decision and quickly caught up with the woman, never losing sight of her. She identified herself and asked for the scarf in the purse. The customer opened her purse and Betty saw the scarf. She listened as the woman informed her she had a receipt and that she simply made her own even exchange (same merchandise, same price, but a different color, she explained).

Betty insisted she must return to the store's office. In the office the scarf was removed as well as a receipt provided by the woman. However, the receipt didn't reflect a purchase of a scarf; it was for other goods. The woman became somewhat hysterical, and while weeping stated she made a mistake, insisting she had a receipt, which must be at home and claimed she could prove it. Betty Johnson had heard this before, and was confident she observed a theft and knew she had a good case. The police were called. The police cited Ms. Jones into court. Subsequently, Ms. Jones, who turned out to be a frequent customer of this chain, produced the receipt and the matter was dismissed.

Analysis: *Obviously, customers shouldn't make their own exchanges, but they do and thus, these kinds of situations occur. Apparently Betty missed (didn't see) the customer pull the scarf out of her purse. Assuming the store agent insists she observed the woman approach the counter, select the scarf, open her purse and place the scarf therein, the eventual production of the receipt could (and in this case did) cast doubt on the agent's version of what happened. This, despite the fact the industry is aware of that strategy wherein shoplifters steal items that match receipts they find or have saved. Here's a scenario that deserves much closer examination in terms of the security department's decision to arrest the woman and involve the police. The* *policy to arrest and refer to the criminal justice system should be flexible and sensitive to the circumstances of each individual situation: Was it really likely this customer would be so shrewd as to "set up" the store? Would it have been more reasonable to have kept the scarf and tell the customer it would be returned to her upon presentation of the receipt and let her go? And here's a case for the value of closed circuit television cameras. Had the cameras captured exactly what the agent reported, the store would have sufficient probable cause to detain and arrest, irrespective of the subsequent production of a receipt.*

☯☯☯☯☯

Scenario 9A: (*Customer's Viewpoint*): Carlos and his wife Maria has immigrated lawfully to the USA three years earlier. Both had jobs but with sending money back to Guatemala, they were struggling financially. Their little boy, Pedro, needed a winter coat, so Carlos devised a plan. Maria wasn't happy about what was going to transpire but Carlos, after all, was her husband and head of the household. They entered the store before sundown and the Southern California temperature was still in the 60's. They each wore a coat but removed the child's sweater, and seated him in the shopping cart infant seat and entered the store. As they selected various items, placing them in the basket, they came to the children's department. Carlos tried a hooded jacket on their child. "I'm not happy with this business of stealing," said Maria in Spanish. "<u>Silencio</u>"! snapped her husband. He didn't have to repeat the fact the store would never miss one small child's jacket and besides, they were spending money in the store right now. He's a hardheaded man who does what he wants, she reflected. So be it. Just protect us, Mother of Jesus.

Resigned to the plan, Maria decided she didn't care for the color and a second jacket, a one-of-a-kind red and blue, was selected and placed on the little fellow; it fit nicely and the child was perfectly happy with his new coat. Carlos looked around carefully. No employees were in sight. Besides, the entire area was jammed with racks of clothing and one couldn't see what another customer was doing just 10 feet away. Carlos cautiously clipped off the price and manufacturer's tickets with his fingernail clipper, crumpled them and held them in his hand before dumping them in a trash container by the food counter. While at the food counter Carlos bought his wife and boy an ice cream cone, and they continued shopping for a few items Maria still had on her list. After paying for their purchases at the checkout stand, they left the store with Pedro still riding in the basket. As they approached the coin-operated airplane ride for children next to the large glass windows, a man blocked the cart and asked to see the receipt for the child's coat. "What receipt?" answered Carlos, as though he had rehearsed this scenario. "The receipt for that jacket the boy's wearing," answered the man. Carlos stiffened in insult, "Sir, I no have a receipt for what friends give to me. The jacket's a gift to my boy, not yours. Children do wear jackets when it's cold. Why do you think that jacket's yours? Do you accuse my boy of stealing jackets?" shouted Carlos.

"Sir, you, your wife and boy must return inside with me and we'll discuss the matter there, not here," said the man who couldn't help but notice a gathering crowd. Carlos shook a finger at the man. "Shame on you for accusing my family of stealing. We're going home and not with you. Who do you think you are.... some kind of police?" At that, the agent produced his badge from his left pocket and announcing he was a security agent, grabbed the basket that Carlos was now trying to steer towards the parking lot. "Hold on now, mister, you're not leaving this store." Carlos reached across his son and struck the man's hand on the edge of the basket, causing the man to release his grip. The agent then seized Carlos' hand and the two fell to the pavement after hitting the plane ride and bouncing off the large window. By this time other employees arrived and subdued Carlos. The family was returned to the office and the police were summoned.

Scenario 9B: (*Employee's Viewpoint*): Marty, an eight-year security veteran with the discount department store, had a reputation for having a "nose" for catching shoplifters. He couldn't explain it, but it was one of those mystical senses that some people have which allows them to tune in on people who have a guilty aura about them...something few enjoy. Most people don't believe in this special sense, but seasoned retail security practitioners suspect it might be true. Marty had noticed the little boy in the shopping cart and wondered why he wasn't wearing a coat. Most everyone was wearing a sweater or jacket, especially children. He thought perhaps the child's sweater or jacket was under the items lying in the basket or out in the car. No big deal. But he did make a mental note of the child not wearing a coat or jacket and continued on in his patrolling of the store. Besides, the child's mother looked like a religious lady with a cross on her necklace. Not that a cross means a hill of beans, thought Marty as his mind flicked through thoughts here and there.

Not fifteen minutes later, he again came upon that same family. The youngster was eating ice cream that was running down the front of what certainly looked like a brand-new jacket. Damn! he exclaimed to himself. Sure as sin they put that jacket on the kid and will push him right out through the check-out stand without paying for it. There wasn't time for him to go searching for the tickets taken off the coat. Even if I had time or someone to help me one of the parents probably ditched them where we couldn't easily find them, he figured. He watched the family purchase their selections and noted their purchases did not include a child's coat. As the parents pushed the basket along the walkway in front of the store, Marty stopped the cart and spoke forcefully and politely, "Excuse me, folks. I work for the store and need to see the receipt for your little boy's jacket." The male parent retorted loudly, "Receipt! What receipt?"

Oh-Oh! thought Marty, Here's a big PR problem. His mind raced. Here I've got a crook in front of me and he knows I didn't see him steal the jacket and I know he knows I didn't see it, but he stole it and I'm sticking with this one. He spoke firmly, "The receipt for the jacket the kid's wearing." The matter went downhill from there, and force was required to return the family and jacket to the office. In the office the man and woman protested their innocence, saying they had proof and a witness who would come forward and testify the jacket had been purchased in a store in the Glendale Mall. The two police officers that responded decided after reviewing the facts and listening to both sides they couldn't issue a citation for theft because a theft couldn't be established. They further agreed to allow the store to keep the jacket in question, pending submission of the proof of ownership, viewing the exchange as a civil matter. They did agree to take a report with respect to the ownership of the coat and the striking of the agent's hand by the customer and submit it to the City Attorney for that office's consideration.

Analysis: *The store security agent clearly erred because he did not observe the selection/taking of the jacket. Although it may seem apparent that a theft occurred, just consider this: Couldn't the child have complained of being cold and the family temporarily interrupted the shopping long enough to just purchase the jacket and then continue with their shopping list? Or couldn't the father or mother have left the store and fetched the jacket from the car? That's why the law requires such certainty when it comes to making arrests. One cannot arrest for a crime unless such crime was committed in the arresting person's presence. That said it was established many months later that the coat had indeed* *been stolen that evening. The friend committed perjury in his testimony about giving the coat as a gift after purchasing it in a specific store in a specific shopping center. (Author's note: The manufacturer of that coat provided evidence that that coat was manufactured for and retailed exclusively by the store in which this incident occurred and could not have been purchased from another company.)*

☯☯☯☯☯

Threats and Promises

Scenario 10A: (*Customer's Viewpoint*): Mrs. Crane picked up both children at the day care center and decided to make a quick stop at the store to purchase her husband a portable TV set for Father's Day. She had seen the ad and the price was compelling. "You're fortunate, madam, this is the last set we have. It was on display and I'll have to get the original carton and accessories... it'll only be a couple minute," said the salesman. "Thank you," she said, as she looked over at the two toddlers who now sat happily on the floor. "Oh, no, no, babies...the floor's dirty. Don't sit there. Mommy will be done in just a couple minutes and we'll go home." Tina started to cry, "I want to go now," she whimpered. "Me, too, mommy. I don't like it here and I'm hungry," said her brother. Mother gave a wane smile, "In a minute, the man will bring us Daddy's present and we'll go home. Don't you want me to get Daddy a present?" "Uh- huh," they both chimed in. "But I'm hungry," repeated Danny, "and I want to go home." "Me hungry, too," echoed Tina, who intentionally plopped back down on the floor and started to cry softly.

The salesman came back to the counter and said, "I'm so sorry, I can't find the power pack to the set. Please bear with me and I'll find it." "Please!" pleaded the woman, now concerned that the children were becoming overtired and the delay was starting to tell on them. Now Danny started whimpering and the two couldn't be quieted or consoled. Mrs. Crane saw a display of packaged candy hanging on a rack across the aisle and thought such a treat might pacify the children until she could conclude her transaction. I'll just take the candy and pay for it when I pay for the TV, she thought. She removed the package of candy, priced at 79 cents and the children calmed down with the treat.

The salesman reappeared, asked for more time, sounding quite frustrated with his inability to locate the battery and again disappeared. After more delays the man finally presented the complete boxed set and even though almost all sales are made at the checkout stands, major purchases such as this are transacted in this big- ticket department to accommodate the customer. He recorded the sale but didn't know about or include the 79-cent candy package. Mrs. Crane by that time had forgotten about the candy and was pleasantly surprised to hear she didn't have to stand in line at the cashier stations at the front of the store. Upon completing the sale the helpful salesman said, "Thank you so much for your patience, Mrs. Crane. Please allow me to carry your purchase to your car." He placed the carton in the basket, along with both children. They by-passed the checkout stands and passed by the store's door greeter. Not far from the door, much to the salesman's surprise and certainly to the agitation of the customer, a gentleman stopped them and after identifying himself as an agent of the Loss Prevention Department, asked Mrs. Crane, "Didn't you forget to pay for something?" "I don't think so," she answered, puzzled by the question. "Does the word "candy' ring a bell?" She looked dazed, then spoke, "Oh my, yes. I'm sorry. I completely forgot about the candy. I'm so sorry."

"Well, we'll give you a chance to fix that, if you'll simply follow me please," and they all returned to the store, pushing the basket. They passed the checkout area where Mrs. Crane could pay for the candy and continued, much to her distress, because the children were starting to become restless again. They reached the rear of the store and entered into the security office. "Why do I have to pay here," she asked, "instead of at the registers in front?" Ignoring her question, the security agent asked for her identification. "Why do you want my identification for me to pay for the candy?" she asked, mystified by the events. The agent held out his hand, expecting the identification. She opened her purse and placed her driver's license in his hand, mostly out of wanting to expedite this matter as quickly as possible.

"Mrs. Crane," commenced the agent, "all I require from you is your signature on this form, admitting the theft, and we'll let you go on your way." "Theft?" she gasped, "what theft?" "Theft of the candy," replied the agent calmly. "We call it theft when you eat our merchandise and don't pay for it. What do you call it?" "I call it a mistake, that's what I call it, and I take great exception, sir, to you suggesting I stole anything. I'm not signing any form that states I stole anything. I want to pay for the candy and leave immediately. My children are tired, I'm tired and I'm leaving. Where do I pay?" The agent was not moved, "Mrs. Crane, you don't understand. You either admit you failed to pay for the merchandise or I'll have no choice but to call the police." "This is outrageous! Let me use your phone to call my husband." "You may not call anyone. Either you sign this admission or I must call the police. And let me point out, Mrs. Crane, if you force me to call the police, they'll have to take your children to the juvenile unit for safekeeping."

Mrs. Crane broke into tears and upon seeing how upset their mother was and seeing her cry, the children also started crying. "My God, what's this all about over some candy?" She turned to the salesman, who was stunned by the events unfolding before him, but was speechless.... it was all beyond him. "This can't be. I can't sign something that isn't true. I didn't try to steal anything. Please, let me call my husband." The agent refused the request again, and in the clamor and crying and near- hysteria, Mrs. Crane signed the form, so she could leave with her children.

Scenario 10B: (*Employee's Viewpoint*): Greta, a relief cashier, had noticed the well-groomed lady with her two little children in the appliance section on her way to the employees' lounge. She even thought to herself how hard it is to shop with such little children. She should have those tikes in day care, if you ask me, she thought to herself. After visiting with co-workers and polishing off a soda, she returned to the front, and there was the same customer. Now the kids were crying. Yeah, see, she confirmed to herself. Then, to her surprise she saw the woman walk over to a candy display fixture, remove a bag of candy, open it and give each child some of the candy. Bet she forgets to pay for that candy, she thought and then, of all people there was the Loss Prevention agent coming around the corner. "Harry," she said, "quick, let me show you a lady who has our candy in her hand which she just took off the rack." Sure enough, Harry could see what Greta was reporting. "How do I know she didn't pay for it?" he asked. Greta responded, "Man, I watched her. She walked right to the fixture and took it. How could she pay back there?" That question sounded reasonable to Harry. "Watch her," Greta said. "I'll bet you she doesn't pay for it." Harry took up the challenge, deciding to maintain constant surveillance to see if the customer was going to pay for the candy or not. A short time later the customer dropped the now-empty cellophane candy bag into a trash container, and Harry recovered it as evidence.

Only big-ticket items could be recorded at the terminal in major appliances, so Harry knew the lady had to go to a front checkout stand to pay for the candy. She didn't, as she and the salesperson by-passed that area as they left the store. This wasn't a risky or complicated matter. The customer admitted outside she hadn't paid for the candy;

that's simple theft. All he had to do to satisfy company policy was to obtain her written admission, which released the store from any liability, and she could leave. To his amazement the customer wouldn't admit to the language on the pre-printed form which read: ".... removed the merchandise from the store without paying for it." He shook his head, "Good grief, the merchandise was in her children's stomachs'. What was so wrong with the language?" All he wanted to do was get the release so they could both go.

Analysis: *Store personnel had every right to stop this customer and ask her to return to the store to pay for the candy. If the store felt some form of release was necessary, then a simple hand-written statement, stating she inadvertently forgot to pay, would have been sufficient, and she could have paid and that would have concluded the incident. If she still refused to even sign a brief statement, the receipt would be a form of documentation and that, coupled with a statement from the salesman who witnessed all this, would have sufficed. This over-eager agent just didn't handle the matter in an appropriate or acceptable fashion and as a consequence, caused a substantial problem for his employer. His insistence was equivalent to threatening the customer with arrest and jail if she refused to sign an admission of theft, which approached extortion. Security personnel cannot, and never should, make any promises or threats in obtaining admissions or any other form of cooperation from a person accused of theft.*

❧❧❧❧❧

Use of Handcuffs and "Use of Force"

Scenario 11A: (*Customer's Viewpoint*): Rose Miller, now 84 years old, knows she should have stopped smoking years ago for two reasons: One, she suffers from emphysema and her doctors have repeatedly told her smoking is aggravating her respiratory problem, and two, her very limited monthly pension check meant good nourishment was sacrificed for the price of cigarettes. So if the occasion allowed, she would just "lift" a pack or two. This Wednesday morning she had a can of tuna fish, crackers, (both of which were on sale) and a small box of her favorite tea in her cart. This was her favorite drug store because they offered a limited supply of grocery items at good prices. With those items and her prescription she carefully approached the cigarette display and, as though she was "just looking," took a pack of Camels from the display. Her large purse was intentionally left wide-open in the child's seat portion of the cart and, looking about, she dropped the pack into the purse. She quickly entered check stand #2 and paid for everything except the cigarettes. Outside, a man from the store stopped her, and she knew she had been busted. She was so embarrassed "Lordy-Lordy, help me through this!" she murmured, fearful the emotional event would trigger another asthma attack. "Madam, I wish you hadn't done this, for your sake as well as mine," said the man, as he escorted her back to the store, slowly, half-embarrassed by the event. At the bottom of the stairs which led to the store's offices she turned to the gentleman and said, "Young man...I don't think ...I can make those stairs...I'm getting so short...of breath all of a sudden. When I get upset and things, my breathing...really acts up. Must we?"

"I'm sorry ma'am, but we must." He nodded, "I'll help you. Just take one step at a time and I'll be right behind you. If it's okay with you, I'll hold your elbow." In the office he said, after determining her name, "Rose, I'm going to have to place these cuffs on you because of company policy but they'll be loose and won't hurt, I'm sorry about this, too." Rose quietly cried, more to herself than out loud. When the police arrived, they ordered the cuffs be removed. Rose was cited for theft and ordered to court. The police assisted her down the stairs after calling a niece who said she'd come and pick up her aunt and drive her home. Later on, based on the encouragement of the niece, a lawsuit was filed against the store for "Excessive Use of Force."

Scenario 11B: (*Employee's Viewpoint*): Glenn rotated among five stores and today was assigned to the "Boulevard" store. The manager really felt his store should be entitled to more security coverage because of the losses, but it wasn't his call. Glenn had come to learn over time that cigarettes were a "hot" theft item...especially among teenagers. Equipped with such insight, he spent a lot of time inconspicuously hovering close to the cigarette display near the entrance to the checkout stands. On this morning he watched an elderly lady push her cart towards the stand and stop near the cigarette display. His "antennae" immediately shot up, because the customer's large, old and funky-looking straw purse was in the child's seat, wide-open, and any passer-by could see all the contents. Lady, he thought, your purse gives your intentions away.

He watched her maneuver her cart almost against the display, which was that much more suspicious, as she looked about to see if anyone might be watching. Sure enough, the lady reached for and took a pack of Camel Longs and dropped them into the yawning purse. Then she quickly pushed the purse down, closing the opening and proceeded to the checkout counter. She did not pay for the cigarettes, as expected. Although he was pleased to catch another customer stealing, the whole purpose of his work, he disliked arresting elderly customers. They're so pathetic, he thought. But, someone has to do it, he resigned to himself. This particular lady posed a problem because she wasn't well. Some months later he learned the handcuffs had badly bruised her wrists, and she claimed some physical disability as a result; he didn't believe that was true. He told friends the store was following a policy in which all detainees were handcuffed to ensure against escape and to protect employees against possible violence.

Analysis: *Detaining this customer was appropriate. If her medical condition was known or the stress of climbing the stairs was observed, it would have been more reasonable or appropriate to handle this matter in some other private area of the store on the* *main floor. If the store personnel were unaware of her condition and the effect of climbing wasn't noticed until arrival on the upper floor, their escorting her to the regularly designated area was appropriate. However, the application of handcuffs once in the office was unnecessary and unreasonable and constituted excessive use of force. A store has every right to adopt and administer a handcuff policy; however, some provisions should be made to allow exceptions to the policy on a case-by-case basis. And good judgment must always be exercised. This lady certainly wasn't about to escape nor did she constitute a threat to employees.*

🐾🐾🐾🐾🐾

Scenario 12A: (*Customer's Viewpoint*): Everyone in the family knew Troy was using drugs and had been when he dropped out of school. "I've lost track of the number of times that boy's been arrested," exclaimed his mother, shaking her head. Troy couldn't help himself. He'd been in a rehab program twice before, but once back on the street with old friends, always resorted to his old habits. Today he needed money again. He'd been lucky a couple times in the fancy department store downtown, so he returned. Troy's appearance was neither remarkable nor suspicious; he didn't look like a misfit as he wandered through the fashion jewelry department. Nice! he thought to himself, spotting a necklace display. Look at those pearls. $199.99! That's worth a couple of rocks in a heartbeat, and I don't even know if they're real or fakes, but who cares? A lady came uncomfortably close, looking at merchandise, so he set the necklace back on the display and walked away, thinking, could be security. The woman moved on, and Troy now knew he would go for the pearls today. He circled back to the display, removed the string of beads and with a quick, easy move dropped them into his coat pocket and headed straight for the exit. He walked quickly along the sidewalk near the parking structure. Then his adrenaline started pumping, because he heard steps gaining on him. He had been down this road before and just knew it was probably store security. He quickened his pace, then heard a woman's voice call out, "Sir, just a moment please, I need to talk to you." Like hell you do, he said to himself, and immediately broke into a fast run. A quick look back over his shoulder revealed a woman chasing him, and she was being passed by a young man...obviously another security agent. The agent grabbed his jacket before they got to the end of the building, slowing down Troy's progress. Troy, almost falling, spun around and swung his fist at the face of the agent, missing its mark. He fell with the agent on top. The woman caught up and he knew he was busted again. He felt the cuffs being ratcheted on his wrists and knew it was over and just went limp. In the security office the security people released the handcuff from his left hand and attached the loose cuff to a metal ring attached to the wall. There he sat with his right hand immobilized, chained to the wall. After the necklace was recovered and the paperwork completed, the police were called. The police arrived 2 ½ hours later. This customer claimed he was held for an excessive and unreasonable period of time and being chained to the wall was barbarous and inhumane treatment.

Scenario 12B: (*Employee's Viewpoint*): "Hey, isn't this the same guy that we were looking at a couple weeks ago?" asked Veronica, as she pointed to the monitor screen covering the fashion jewelry. "Yeah, I remember that little ponytail," replied Red, Veronica's assistant. "Yeah, and I'm sure he got us for something in the gift department, too, but I lost sight of him for a minute so had to let him walk," mused Veronica. "Isn't it funny how they always seem to come back if they score?" "Uh-huh, but I'm not sure they come back because success breeds confidence in their skills or success breeds contempt for our skills!" observed Veronica in a stage whisper. "Anyhow," she said loudly, "he's mine today." Jill, the rookie agent, was at the desk reviewing the procedure and policy manual.

"Jill," called the security manager, "come here and stay with this jerk with the ponytail. We're going down to work him close, because this kind of guy moves fast when he's got what he wants. You're probably going to see another take. Remember, watch the hands, not the face. The hands do the stealing." As it turned out, Jill clearly observed the subject pick up a necklace, replace it and walk away, return within three minutes, again pickup the same necklace and the hand holding the necklace went in and out of his jacket pocket so fast, that had she blinked, she would have missed it. "Wow!" she almost shouted into the radio, "He took the necklace and it's in his right jacket pocket." "I saw it, too," came Veronica's voice over the radio. Jill watched the shoplifter exit through the parking side doors, followed by Veronica and several seconds later, joined by Red. In the office the pony-tailed detainee denied ever being in the store before, denied ever shoplifting, denied using drugs and denied he attempted to hit Red with his fist. When two police officers eventually arrived, the corporal looked at the prisoner and said, "Don't we know one another? Troy, isn't it? Troy, my man, when are you ever going to get the message?"

Analysis: *Once a customer has demonstrated the propensity for resistance and violence, as in this case, keeping him contained and subdued in handcuffs is customary and reasonable. A store has three choices: (1) Keep the person cuffed with their hands behind their back; (2) keep the person cuffed with their hands in front; or (3) cuff one hand to a fixed object. The first is uncomfortable (if not painful) and the second can be dangerous because the cuffed hands can be used as a weapon. Securing the shoplifter to the fixed object (or wall ring) allows them to sit in relative comfort; hence, it's the most humane.*

With respect to the issue of an excessive period of time, it's known in the industry that police response to retailers' request for assistance in terms of transporting a shoplifter to jail, is notoriously slow. In the police defense, however, shoplifting is a low police priority. Interestingly, a claim that a retailer had held a shoplifter for an excessive period of time is really restricted or limited to the time between *apprehension and <u>the time the police were called</u>. This delay is also unwelcome by the store because the security agent is then "out of service" waiting for the police to arrive and take the shoplifter away. Put another way, agents are not out on the selling floor productively engaged in conducting their profession...that is watching out for more shoplifters.*

☙☙☙☙☙

Fitting Rooms and Searches

Scenario 13A: (*Customer's Viewpoint*): Well, if I can't find it in this store, then I give up, thought the young woman wearing a stylish blazer and plaid skirt. With her purse hanging on her arm, she quickly scooted the hangers around the round rack of blouses and pulled three blouses out to try on. I don't know why long sleeves are so limited in my size, she thought. Absent any sales help, she carried her selections into the fitting room. Stacie thought the pale blue blouse might work but the other two wouldn't do at all, so she carried them out and laid them on the counter. She went back to the rack and selected three more blouses, returned to the same fitting room and went through the process of buttoning, unbuttoning and looking in the mirror. Darn it, she thought, please don't let this whole afternoon be for nothing. Then she returned the three blouses to the counter and selected the last three in her size on the rack. The cream-colored one with the ruffles in the front looked just right. So she went out to the counter, gathered up all the blouses and quickly tossed them over the rack used for unselected items, assuming a clerk would re-hang all of them. She carried her one selection to the wrap station and paid for it with her store charge card. As she stepped off the curb, a casually dressed young woman wearing a sweatshirt, jeans and tennis shoes stopped her and after identifying herself as a Loss Prevention Agent for the store, told her she wanted Stacie to return to the store to "discuss a problem."

"What kind of problem?" demanded Stacie. "The problem of the blouse you haven't paid for," answered the agent. "I paid for my blouse. What are you talking about?" protested the customer. "I'm sorry," insisted the employee, "You must come back inside with me. Please don't make me force you to do it," warned the agent. Confused and trying to think what she could have done to bring on this situation, Stacie accompanied the employee. Inside the young woman asked if she could look into her two sacks containing purchases she made that afternoon. "Well, where's the light-blue blouse?" asked the agent. The questions and answers obviously didn't satisfy the agent, who asked a colleague in the office to stay with her. The agent disappeared for 10 minutes, then reappeared in the office and stated, "I know you have the blue blouse. It must be under your clothing. Why don't you just give it to me so we can stop playing games."

Stacie responded, "Lady, I don't have your blouse it certainly isn't under my clothing. Either you let me go or I'm going to walk out of here. Either that or call the police." "I'll be glad to call the police because they'll search you and when they recover the blouse, you'll be booked for theft. We don't need to involve the police, if you'll only cooperate with me, and remove your blazer and give me the blouse," insisted the agent. "Call the police, I said," shouted Stacie, "I don't have your damn blouse and enough's enough." The police, with a community storefront office in the shopping center, were called and responded quickly. "We can't search this customer unless she's under arrest for theft," stated the senior of the two police officers. "Is she under arrest?" "Yes," replied the agent. The female police officer took the customer into a private area and determined the customer had no stolen or hidden merchandise. The police also informed the store manager that the agent had not established a crime and must release the customer. Stacie left...angrily vowing to sue the store.

Scenario 13B: (*Employee's Viewpoint*): Debbie hadn't made an apprehension in over a week and was becoming frustrated. She had just spent almost an hour on two teenagers whom she knew were going to steal, but they did not. As she was about to leave the area, an attractive woman entered hurriedly, looking in all directions, one of the signs of a shoplifter. Shoplifters can't help that trait; after all, one must know if they're being observed or not. No one is going to be so foolish as to steal with a witness watching.

The lady selected three blouses, too quickly to suit Debbie's taste, another characteristic of a retail thief, i.e., they aren't as careful about their selection because they're not going to be paying for it. Okay, she took three items in. Let's see what she brings out, said Debbie to herself. Within a few minutes the customer came out of the fitting room with two blouses. There's still one in there or under her clothing, calculated the agent. The customer re-entered the same fitting room with three more blouses. Several minutes later the lady emerged from Room #4 carrying three items, selected three more and re-entered the fitting room. Debbie watched the lady finally carry out two blouses in one hand and one in the other, pick up the others and tossed them over the rack. As the lady walked down the fitting room hallway, Debbie, who posed as a customer carrying several garments into the adjacent fitting room, quickly looked into Room #4 and noted there were no items left behind. She's still got one! she thought. Debbie watched the customer purchase one blouse and then leave the store. Outside, the customer denied stealing or having stolen merchandise, a not uncommon reaction. In the office the customer refused to allow her to look under her clothing and her hand was forced.

Debbie knew she had to either let the woman walk or call her bluff and call the police. She knew she had accounted for all the items and was confident the woman had guts and was going to push her to the limit. Okay, lady, I'll call your bluff, she thought to herself, knowing full well if she was wrong, it could be disastrous. But, before calling the police, she asked her partner to watch the customer, so she could double check for the light blue-blouse that was never returned. She ran back to the department and to dressing Room #4;

it was empty, no merchandise. She looked in the Rooms #3 and #5, just in case the customer set her up by hiding a garment to force an arrest. No items. She returned to the round rack from which all the blouses had been selected and didn't see the blue one. She has to have it under her clothing and I'm going all the way on this one, she determined while returning to the security office.

When it was all over and the police and customer were gone, she sat in disbelief. She mentally reviewed, step by step, the entire transaction and couldn't find where she had made a mistake. As required by policy she called her regional security manger and reported the bad stop and subsequently wrote as detailed a report as she could. The only possible explanation, she finally admitted, was that her count was flawed, that the blue blouse was probably somehow folded with another blouse and simply not visible.

Analysis: *Fitting rooms are a popular places for stealing merchandise because of the expectation of privacy; security employees know that. Security agents typically use the "count system"(3 items in- --3 items out, etc., etc.) as did this agent, but she was hasty, careless or not thorough in accounting for all the items, convinced this customer was guilty of theft. Nothing the customer did would rise to the level of "probable cause." It's not uncommon for customers to trek in and out of fitting areas, trying on items in their effort to make the right selection. The mistake was compounded by her persistence and calling the police. Searching can be a humiliating event, and people who are subjected to* *searches under their clothing, more often than not, are outraged.*

Now, customers are not guaranteed absolute and total privacy inside a fitting room. Many rooms have curtains over the door or have louvered doors through which any person can see into the room. Other customers, employees and security agents can see and do see into the rooms through the openings so afforded, and that's not illegal. Use of video cameras or other devices such as vents or grills is prohibited.

☯☯☯☯☯

Scenario 14A: (*Customer's Viewpoint*): Holly had long raven hair pulled back into a single braid, beautiful dark eyes and a sleek figure to match her beautiful face. No question, she turned heads wherever she went. It was August, and the beaches were jammed with tourists. As usual, Holly, one of those vacationing in the area had her favorite place on the beach and, as usual, had a group of admirers who looked for her each late morning. The trouble was, her inventory of beachwear needed help. She entered the store with one thing in mind, I need another swimsuit.

She took two one-piece swimsuits and two bikini-style suits and in the privacy of the fitting room, tried on all four. Oh, I hate myself for not being able to make a decision, she thought. "Morning, honey," said a sales employee, as Holly took two of the suits back out to exchange for more choices. "Is there anything I can help you with?" "No, I'm just going to try another one or two. If I need you, I'll let you know." She selected one more one-piece suit and returned to the room. She again tried on the first two and then her most recent selection. She partially exited the bank of fitting rooms to see who was in the area. As she peered out onto the selling floor, she noted the one helpful salesperson was at the cashier station, busily engaged with another customer. Holly returned to the room and put on the black one-piece suit and slipped into her skirt and blouse and beach cover-up. The suit was completely concealed. Like taking candy from a baby, she mused with a smile on her face. She gathered up her store bag and beach bag, left the other suits lying about the room and brazen-ly walked out of the area onto the selling floor...on through the department, passing the clerk who smiled at her...and out the door. At the sidewalk a young woman who was similarly dressed in colorful and airy summer attire confronted her. "Excuse me, miss, but I'm a security employee with Sonteal's and I need to talk to you about a swimsuit. Would you please come back to the store for a minute?"

"What swimsuit?" asked Holly, with a notice-able crack in her voice. "A swimsuit I need to locate with your assistance," said the woman who now stood close to Holly. "In fact, may I look in your bag?" "No," said Holly, her mind racing as to what she should say or do, "Oh, well, go ahead, look, look all you want," she said, pushing her store bag out while holding it open for the employee. The woman looked without touching the contents of the bag, then asked, "And your beach bag?" Holly, now believing she could be out of the woods on this if she showed the store detective the inside of her beach bag, held it open. "There," said Holly, "are you satisfied?" "I'm sorry," said the woman, "You must come back. We can't settle this out here," The woman obviously meant business, so Holly, re-entered the store with her and went into a private office. Inside the office the security employee looked straight at Holly and asked, "What's your first name?" "Holly," was her answer. "Holly, are you wearing one of our swimsuits under your cloth-ing?" "I certainly am not," she snapped, with as much emphasis as she dared use.

"All right, have it your way," said the agent. "Please give me your identification, and would you kindly hand me your beach cover-up and we'll put it over the chair here." Holly complied.

After she finished examining the driver's license and other documents, the agent dropped the wallet, scattering its contents on the floor, exclaiming, "Oh, I'm sorry!" Both women bent down to the floor to pick up the items. While Holly was bent down, the agent stood up and lifted the back of Holly's blouse, exposing the black swim-suit. "Well, well," chirped the agent, "What have we here?" Holly stood up and confronted the agent. "How dare you look under my blouse?" "How dare you come into this store and attempt to steal our merchandise?" retorted the detective. The police were summoned, and Holly admitted she was attempting to steal the swimwear but claimed the employee looking under her blouse violated her rights. She was transported to the local police station and with the assistance of female officers, the stolen merchandise was recov-ered and taken into evidence.

Scenario14B: (*Employee's Viewpoint*): Every security agent has a favorite methodology of picking out likely subjects to follow. Kate's was most comfortable in watching customers entered through the main doors of the store and from among those, arbitrarily selecting the one to watch. She'd follow for a short while and if nothing of interest developed, she'd disengage the surveillance and then start all over again. Part of the reason for this method was her understanding that a survey conducted some years back disclosed that one out of every ten customers either shoplifted or attempted to shoplift. So she had decided to play the averages. What a striking beauty! she thought to herself, as she watched a young woman enter, her long black hair pulled back into a braid. I'll stay with you for a bit, Ms. State Beauty Queen, she thought, as she followed the girl to the swimwear department. She positioned herself where she could clearly observe the customer select four swimsuits and then enter the bank of fitting rooms. She followed close enough to know the customer was in Room #5.

Shortly thereafter the customer left the room with two of the four items, had a brief discussion with Mrs. Kelley of that department, and returned to Room #5 with one item. Five minutes later the woman exited the room nervously and tip-toed to the entrance from the selling floor, cautiously looked out, then quickly returned to Room #5. Yes, oh yes, she thought. This one's beauty is only skin deep.... she's going to take. Then she spoke one word into her radio, "Yoshi." "Yoshi, here" came an immediate response. Kate responded,

"Come to Department 56 quick. I think we have a live one."

Yoshi arrived within seconds and was quickly appraised of the situation. She was instructed to maintain surveillance on the beauty when she exited the fitting rooms while Kate inspected Room #5 to account for a total of three items. If the customer returned all three to the selling floor or left the three in the room, the surveillance would be discontinued. Between the two security employees they should be able to account for all the suits. If all three couldn't be accounted for, then the customer had to have one somewhere in her possession or on her person. Pretty standard. Yoshi also knew her task thereafter was to follow at a distance in the event of violence and to remain in the background until all parties were in the office. When the beauty left Room #5, Kate spoke quietly into her radio, "Here she comes: light summer flower pattern skirt and top with white beach cover-up, long black braided hair...she's carrying a Green's bag and a beach bag, no suits in sight." "10-4," replied Yoshi. "She's yours for the next 60 seconds, baby," whispered Kate again, who by this time had pushed past the curtain enclosing the fitting room and observed only two swim suits. She took one! she thought to herself. "I'm missing one suit," she radioed to Yoshi. It was up to Yoshi now. Yoshi had to watch the customer to observe if she would approach a salesperson and produce a suit, or dispose of a suit because she changed her mind about shoplifting it, or complete the act of theft by exiting the store. As the customer was about to exit thorough the doors, Kate had left the fitting room bank and was also confirming with Yoshi that the customer had not purchased or disposed of a suit. "She's all yours," said Yoshi, "and I'm on your tail."

Kate hurried toward the customer. "Excuse me, miss. I'm with Sonteal's Security Department and I need to talk to you about a swimsuit. Please return to the store with me." The customer denied any knowledge of a swimsuit; in fact, she voluntarily opened a store sack she was carrying as well as her beach bag. But Kate knew by the expression on the woman's face she was guilty...knew it from years of experience. Kate returned the woman to the office, followed at a distance by Yoshi. In the office the customer still maintained ignorance of any suit to the point that it was embarrassing. You think I fell off a turnip truck? Kate thought to herself. When the customer leaned over to pick up her effects from the floor, Kate peeked under the back of the customer's blouse and there it was! The police were called and transported the customer to the station. Later Kate was advised the prosecutor's office had varying opinions about the legality of Kate's "search."

The issue in question had to do with the admissibility of evidence with a central question: If the search had been conducted by the police, would it be admissible and was Kate's search legal or illegal? Their final decision was they would not pursue the matter with a prosecution but opined the store's detention was legal.

Analysis: *Security employees should never conduct body or personal searches of any suspected*

*shoplifter. If a customer is suspected of having mer-
chandise secreted under their clothing, they should
be asked to surrender it and given the privacy to do
so. If the party denies having the merchandise and
the security agent is convinced it's there (perhaps a
tag is showing or because of the bulky outline) and
refuses to surrender the merchandise, the police
should be called to conduct the search.*

❧❧❧❧❧

EAS (Electronic Article Surveillance Systems) & Searches

Scenario 15A: (*Customer's Viewpoint*): Mrs.
Jackson had completed her last purchase, and
Clarissa had gotten away from her again as she
gathered up her bags. "Clarissa," she called out.
The toddler re-appeared from behind a pillar mis-
chievously. "Shame on you, baby. I told you not to
leave Mama," as she reached down with her free
hand and took the three-year-old's hand. The
youngster laughed at being scolded, and they
headed for the door. As they exited the store, a
bell sounded. Mrs. Jackson realized the device
was reacting to her, so she stopped, turned
around, backing away from the store's entrance,
not knowing what she should or shouldn't do.
Within seconds a uniform security officer came up
to her and spoke crisply. "Please return and step
through the sensors again, madam." She obligingly walked back into the store, turned and exited
again, with no alarm sounding either time. "Have
your little girl step through now," said the guard.

Upon entering the store, the child's passage through the sensors sounded the bell. Her mother called the child back and again the alarm sounded. "We'll have to go to the office, lady," announced the guard. Mrs. Jackson and the child rode the escalator down, followed by the officer. "You'll have to search your daughter to see what she has under her clothing," said the guard.

Mrs. Jackson began to get irritated, "My child has nothing. Why look at her, man! She's a baby. Do you really think she stole something? " "Lady, the alarm isn't going off for no reason. Either you must search her or I will. It's not like she's a grown woman, you know." "Well, I'm not searching that child. So you better do what you got to do Mister, because we've got to be going," stated Mrs. Jackson, feeling somewhat helpless in the presence of this official, along with being mystified as to why Clarissa had set off the alarm. The guard, in the presence of the mother, unbuttoned the back of the child's dress and by looking down the youngster's now-open dress was able to see her little buttocks as outlined in her panties. Then, after a cursory check with his hand inside the dress around her waistline in front, he quickly withdrew his hand. It was obvious the child had no item or article that could active the alarm. "Well, I don't know how to explain this one," sighed the guard. "Sorry to inconvenience you, madam. You're right. Your daughter doesn't have anything. But you should know that some folks put things in children's clothing and if they get caught they blame the kid. I hope you understand." "The only thing I understand is that probably innocent people can be inconvenienced and embarrassed by your equipment and I'm not going to risk this again by coming here." Later, when Mrs. Jackson described what had happened at the store, her friends and relatives expressed outrage over a store guard's looking inside the girl's dress.

Scenario 15B: (*Employee's Viewpoint*): Guard Williams, an employee of the Sun Star Security Services Company, had been assigned to this store only two days. Since no regular security employees worked for the store, they contracted with Sun Star. The manager cut short Williams' orientation to the store by one of the assistant mangers because he wanted to review an incoming shipment with that assistant. But Williams had worked in other retail stores before, even though they didn't have EAS systems in place. He just assumed that whenever the alarm sounded, it meant something had on one of those alarm tags, which should be removed when the item was purchased. If the tag was still on the merchandise, that meant the article had not been paid for. He was near the front end of the store when he heard the alarm go off. That's the first time I've heard that since I've been here, he thought, ...wonder who handles that?

A cashier looked at him and waved towards the lady customer with the child. Williams interpreted that wave to mean it was his job. He approached the customer who asked, "Why did that go off?" "Well, "just go through it again and we'll see," said Williams, confident that the solution to this problem would present itself. The lady walked in and out without the alarm sounding.

"Okay, please have the youngster walk through it," he requested; that made sense to him. The child set off the alarm twice. "We'll have to go to the office," said Williams, half- wishing someone in authority would appear on the scene and relieve him of a matter for which he had no experience at all. I'm sure the mom will have the kid surrender whatever she has that's setting off the alarm, he hopefully thought to himself. In the office the lady wasn't very understanding as to the problem and in fact refused to surrender anything or even search what the child might have. Seeing no alternative than to unbutton the little girl's dress, he did just that and could see there was nothing hidden. To complete the inspection, he ran his hand through the opened back of her dress and moved his hand around to the girl's tummy. "Nothing. Well, I don't know how to explain this," he said. "I'm sorry to inconvenience you, madam. Very sorry." At this point the large woman bumped him aside as he was fumbling with the buttons, and completed the task of re-buttoning the child's dress herself and they left.

William didn't know what to do next, so he found an assistant manager, in fact, the same one who had started giving him his instructions the day before. He told her the alarm went off, but there was no stolen merchandise involved. To his relief she didn't ask him for any details and he wasn't about to volunteer what happened. The next day Williams was told by his supervisor at Sun Star Security he would not be assigned to that store again because the manager had received a customer complaint about his searching the child.

"Why did you do that, anyway?" asked the security supervisor. William snapped in frustration, "What the hell would you have done when the kid kept setting off the alarm? Act like you didn't hear it?" The supervisor didn't answer and after an awkward pause, they focused on William's new assignment for the day.

Analysis: *Just because an EAS alarm sounds doesn't necessarily mean someone is in the process of stealing. These systems are not really designed to catch crooks; they're designed to discourage or prevent people from shoplifting. They can be used as an important loss prevention tool, yet they're not infallible. And this case is an example of an alarm sounding with no explanation. Such things as proximity access cards and garage door openers can activate the alarm. Security employees should not be involved in responding to these alarms. Sales associates or mangers should respond and inquire. They should ask such questions as to what could the customer possibly be carrying that could active this electronic system. The employee can explain an item just purchased that the salesperson forgot to remove or de-activate the EAS ticket or tag is a common cause of alarms, and explore that possibility. Absent any easily identified cause, allow the customer to proceed. Unless other circumstances are present, I would discourage "patting down" or searching a customer ... "probable cause" not withstanding.*

Another equally important message here has to do with the proper orientation of and instructions given to security personnel, especially temporary and contractual personnel. Too often, store management fails to prioritize its many tasks. So in this case a new shipment was more important than giving the new security officer instructions as to what the store expected him to do. It's better to have no security than to put a security person to work without proper orientation and training.

☯☯☯☯☯

Scenario 16A: (*Customer's Viewpoint*): The annual sweater sale always attracted a rush when the store opened in the morning, Nancy, a local county employee, had arranged to arrive at work late, just so she could be there. At the counter she quickly found the sizes she wanted and grabbed seven. These sweaters were always good gifts for her sister and mother, and she herself wore sweaters to work regularly in the planning department. A special checkout stand had been set up to accommodate the expected crowd of shoppers and the extra sales help was busy. Most customers purchased several sweaters, not just one or two. The price was that attractive. Nancy's turn arrived and she approached the cashier with her armload of colorful sweaters. The cashier scanned one sweater at a time, removed the EAS tags and folded each garment. With interruptions, questions, some difficulty in removing one tag, Nancy noticed that one sweater might not have been scanned. Should I say something or should I just let it go? She worried to herself. She decided to say nothing and let events unfold as they may. If the error were caught, it wouldn't be her fault, she rationalized.

Nervous about the sensors at the front doorway, she purposefully walked to the parking lot exit, but sensors were there, too. She returned to the mall entrance and with a beating heart walked through the sensors, thinking, If it goes off, I can tell them I purchased seven and it's their mistake. She jumped as the alarm sounded and thought to herself, I'll just act innocent and irritated and stand right here. A store supervisor approached her and in a very accommodating voice asked if she would kindly walk through the sensors again. She did and the alarm, as she anticipated, sounded again. In a pleasant voice he asked her what she had purchased. "I bought seven sweaters. I'm one of your store's best fans during the sweater sale," she replied (while cussing herself for even attempting this charade.) Near the sensors was a counter where the two chose to examine the contents of the bag. She removed the nicely folded sweaters and as she had stated, there were seven. The employee looked at the receipt. "My," he stated in a questioning voice, "your receipt only reflects six sweaters." "Well, I paid for seven or at least I thought I was paying for seven," she said defensively, now examining each sweater. "Here's the culprit," said the employee. "This one still has the tag attached." "I hope you're not suggesting I was trying to take this sweater without paying for it, are you?" She pretended to sound part angry and part hurt. "Of course not, not at all," he replied. She tried another ploy. "I can point out the cashier who rang up this transaction and you can ask her if I didn't put all these sweaters on the stand." "There's no need to do that," he said, "Do you still want this sweater?"

"Oh, of course I do," she replied. "Okay, let's take it over to this register. We'll get the tag off, and you can purchase it there. I'm sorry for the inconvenience." She purchased the sweater, and the employee thanked her for her understanding. She acknowledged his thanks and tried to appear a bit miffed. She left the store, not worried about a bell sounding on this trip. That weekend she composed a letter to the store manager, telling him how embarrassing the incident had been, how it was the store's fault, and how she was worried someone may have witnessed this incident.

Scenario 16B: (*Employee's Viewpoint*): Bob Swann was working in his first management post since being elevated from the fast-track trainee squad comprised of university graduates who are recruited for careers in retailing. It was not required, but everyone knew if Bob were in the area when an EAS alarmed, he would be willing to handle it. He even liked dealing with the problem because it was a challenge. The alarm caught his attention, and he approached the customer with a friendly smile. Her facial expression gave him no clue as to her guilt or innocence. "Good morning," he greeted her, almost laughing, "Why don't you walk through the gates again to be sure it knows what it's doing." She did and the alarm sounded again. "What did you purchase?" he asked. "Sweaters, sale sweaters. Seven of them" she responded. He asked for the store sack and stuck it into the alarm field. The alarm sounded. He shook his head. "Let's go over here and see if we can't find the trouble-maker in the bag." They both stood before a nearby counter, where Bob removed the seven neatly folded sweaters. Among the merchandise was a receipt, and Bob noted only six sweaters were itemized on the ticket. Inspection of the sweaters revealed a blue one with an EAS tag still attached.

She offered to identify the cashier, but he knew there would be no point in confronting the cashier. Even if the cashier could remember, what would she say? She failed to ring one sweater? Or the cashier would say she rang everything the customer presented, which would only suggest the customer stuck an additional sweater into the bag after the purchase. If so, then what would he do? So, Bob opted for the best course of action: "Obviously, the girl just missed this one sweater. You still want it, don't you?" he asked. "Of course I do," replied the customer. He went to get a salesperson's assistance to negotiate the sale and the customer finally left. Bob suspected the customer knew that an unpaid-for item was in the bag. But at least he and the EAS system prevented a loss and accommodated a sale.

Analysis: *The store has the right to inquire when an EAS sensor alarms. The customer was never accused of theft. The employee's inquiry was reasonable and polite. The discovery of an item not paid for would suggest the customer was caught in an act of theft, and if that thought crossed the employee's mind he never let on. It was a delicate matter handled professionally and with great diplomacy. The customer knew the cashier couldn't throw any light on why one sweater hadn't been recorded* *and felt the best course of action, particularly to prove she had no evil intentions, was to purchase the sweater now. Indeed, that had been her intention all along. The customer did not have to buy the sweater. She could have said she was angry that she had been stopped because of an employee's error and no longer wanted the sweater and walk away.*

❧❧❧❧❧

Scenario 17A: (*Customer's Viewpoint*): Jerome had just finished working out at the YMCA gymnasium and was going to meet his brother at McDonald's. When the "walk" sign illuminated, he started to step off the curb at the corner in front of the drug store when he felt a hand on his shoulder. Thinking it was one of his gym friends, he stopped and turned, only to see a middle-aged Hispanic gentleman and a husky redhead right behind him. The Hispanic man said, "Excuse me, sir, but I need to look into your bag." "Why in the world do you want to look in my bag?" asked Jerome incredulously. "Well, a good customer tells us she saw you putting our merchandise in your bag there." Jerome bristled and spoke sharply, "And just where in the hell did your lady say she saw me doing this?" "At the CD display in the store, of course," replied Carlos. "Well, your lady customer must be smoking dope "cause I ain't even been in your store, man, and no way you're looking in my bag." He started to continue on his way across the street.

The red-headed man grabbed the strap of Jerome's gym bag and jerked Jerome backwards off balance. Jerome, from this awkward position, spat in the redhead's face, and the redhead promptly retaliated with a punch to Jerome's nose. Blood shot out. Jerome aimed a kick at Carlos, missing the man's groin. The three ended up on the sidewalk with a crowd quickly gathering. A policeman, who happened to be in the area, pushed through the crowd and separated the combatants. The store manager told the cop that Jerome was a shoplifter, had been seen stuffing CD's in his bag and the boy had refused to cooperate. Jerome told the cop he had just been working out in the gym and had never even been inside the store. With Jerome's permission, the policeman looked in the gym bag to discover soiled clothing, but no merchandise. The redhead said he wanted the policeman to arrest Jerome for spitting in his face, and Jerome wanted the policeman to arrest the redhead for punching his face. The policeman said no one was going to be arrested, that it was a matter the detectives would have to sort through and his report would be filled at the station later that day. Jerome subsequently filled a civil action against the store.

Scenario 17B: (*Employee's Viewpoint*): The store manger answered the page: "Carlos," said the pharmacist into the phone. "There's a customer standing in front of me at this moment who tells me she just watched a young black man in a green shirt stuffing CDs into a duffel bag in aisle #11." Carlos put down a shipping document and quickly returned to the selling floor, meeting his red-headed assistant, Buck, at the swinging doors. "Come on," he said to the assistant. "We've got a young black in a green shirt stealing CD's." Buck did a quick about-face and followed his manager. Aisle #11 was void of customers. All the other aisles were checked, and no person fitting the description was seen inside the store. Anxious to catch whoever this thief was, Carlos looked out through the large plate glass window at the front of his store and to his relief there was their culprit, a young black man wearing a green T-shirt, carrying a canvas gym bag. The two store executives ran out the door and got the young man's attention, just before he was about the cross the street with the green light. "Excuse me, young fellow, but I need to take a quick look in your bag," said Carlos. "What for?" asked the youth, stepping backwards to put more distance between him and these two men who were obviously focused on him. "A lady's reported to us that she saw you stealing some of our merchandise," answered Carlos. "Well, go tell the lady she's full of it," said the boy, and started to pass by the two and cross the street. "And you ain't looking in my bag, either." Buck reached out and seized the strap of the gym bag. The boy turned and spit at him. In instant reaction, Buck struck the spitter in the face with his fist. The boy started kicking, and all three fell to the sidewalk. A police officer passing by noted the disturbance and promptly intervened. His on-the-spot investigation disclosed the young black man had been the victim of mistaken identity, and all three had sustained minor injuries.

Analysis: *The store manager and his assistant should never have left the store and should not have* confronted the young man. Further, once the young man denied them access to his bag and started to leave, he should not have been seized and turned around, because there was no probable cause to justify the confrontation and any use of force. Had the original customer who witnessed the stealing been there and pointed out the boy as the shoplifter, an argument could be made that probable cause existed by virtue of an actual eyewitness, and a reasonable investigation could be launched; but that didn't occur here. The management employees assumed this was the shoplifter based on a vague description and went too far. Spitting on another is one form of a criminal assault; as emotionally upsetting and disgusting as that may be, it doesn't warrant a store executive striking another in the face.

☯☯☯☯☯

Merchandise Displayed Beyond the Registers

Scenario 18A: (*Customer's Viewpoint*): The Green's were completing their weekly grocery shopping. The shopping cart, with Carey still seated in the seat and Jeb who was anxiously waiting for the promised stick of gum, once it was paid for, stood by his mother's side. "You sure this is all we need, honey?" she asked. "Yep," replied Mr. Green, then paused, "Oops, I take that back. We need a box of fire logs. Include them in the total bill, and I'll go ahead and get 'em. I'm getting the store brand, not the expensive ones." He left his wife and kids to conclude their purchases and write the check from her checkbook. He walked along the front end of the market to where the fire logs, fire starters, and bar-b-que merchandise was displayed. Before he picked up the box, he went to the entrance to move the car closer to the doors, then changed his mind, returned to the displayed boxes and picked up his selection. He walked through the double entry doors carrying the carton. As he approached the trunk of his car parked in the lot he heard someone say, "One minute there, sir. We need to talk with you." Hank Green completely ignored the voice, believing someone else was been spoken to, not him. No one had any reason to talk to him. The next thing he knew, two men were standing next to him. He had balanced the heavy carton on the car's bumper and opened the trunk lid. One man was now pushing the lid down, not all the way but down far enough so he couldn't put his carton in the trunk. "Sir," said the taller of the two men, "those logs haven't been paid for. Wouldn't you like to pay for them first, before you put them in your car?"

"Well, I beg your pardon," said Hank. "It so happens my wife just paid for them." "Sorry," said the employee. "That story won't work and you'll have to return to the store with that merchandise." Hank frowned, "I'm not returning to the store and I'm not carrying this heavy box back inside, either. I'm telling you my wife's paid for this and she'll be here in a minute with my children." Hank was getting angry now. The store agent persisted. "Mister, either you come now like a gentleman or we'll have do it the hard way. Which do you prefer?" Hank, now looking aggressive, said, "Back off, buster. This is paid for, and it's mine. I told you I'm not going back. Get out of my face and go get your manager."

The two agents saw the man clenching his right fist. The next thing Hank knew he was on the ground and cuffs were being used to secure his wrists. He was helped to his feet and escorted back. He had struck his head on the pavement and was stunned over the swiftness and startlingly suddenness of his predicament. "Let me go you sons-of-bitches!" he kept shouting, causing everyone in the lot to turn and look. Mrs. Green, preoccupied with giving gum to Jeb, pushed past the customers who were peering at some disturbance ahead of her and saw her husband being escorted through a solid door and shouting. Greatly alarmed, she pushed the basket up to the door and banged on it, while trying to keep track of Jeb at the same time. With no response to her banging, she took a can of vegetables and used it to hit the door; it opened and a man snapped at her, "What're you doing lady?"

"That's my husband you have in there," she screeched. "What's going on in there?" "He's under arrest for shoplifting," was the curt answer to her question. "Shoplifting!" she exclaimed, "Shoplifting what?" "He was caught with a carton of fire logs," said the man. "I paid for those logs," she shouted, "I've got a receipt for the logs. You've made a horrible mistake." "Where's your receipt?" asked the man. She quickly pulled the long ribbon of a receipt from her purse and handed it to the man, who was only part-way out of the room. She could still hear her husband and then Jeb started crying. The man stepped out, closed the door and said, "There's no fire logs on this receipt. Why would you tell me that?" With a quizzical look, she shouted, "Ask the clerk. I paid for 'em!"

The security man, followed by Mrs. Green and Jeb, returned to the cashier. The cashier said, "Oh Lord, she did tell me to add the logs and I simply forget. It's my fault." The handcuffs were removed from Mr. Green with profuse apologies. He was asked why he refused to cooperate. His response was terse, "Why were you in such a big hurry to get me back in the store when I told you my wife would be coming soon?"

Scenario 18B: (*Employee's Viewpoint*): Andy was in training and working alongside Mitch Mc-Pherson. The two had been out in Mitch's car, going through a chapter in the company's security manual. As they re-entered through the west door, they found themselves following a man in a red and black plaid shirt who walked the length of the front part of the store. The man slowed down at the bar-b-que area, looked around, started to exit the store through the east doors, then quickly turned and returned to the bar-b-que area and picked up a carton of fire logs. He then promptly walked out of the store. "See, Andy, it can happen right under your nose," said Mitch, half-way startled himself over such a fortuitous crime occurring right in front of him while training a new agent. "Wow! That's pretty simple," said Andy. "Most thefts are not quite that simple to observe," replied the senior man, "That's where luck comes in. Sometimes you're lucky and BAM!... you get one clean as a whistle. Other times you can go for days to the point where you end up praying for a shoplifter." These words were exchanged in hushed tones as the two headed toward the man, who was now trying to open the trunk of his car while balancing the box on the bumper.

"One minute there, sir. We need to talk with you," said Mitch. The man seemed to ignore him. Now alongside, Mitch, unable to resist a little humor in his work, said, "Sir, wouldn't you rather pay for the merchandise before you take it home?" The man isn't in the mood for humor, thought Mitch. The man answered, "My wife's paid for these logs and I'm not going back into the store. Let's wait for her here." Mitch, hating to be lied to about some "mysterious wife" whom he never saw, and anxious not to look too unprofessional in front of this trainee, took command of the situation in a no-nonsense way, when the man used mild profanity in his refusal to cooperate and started to clench his fist. Mitch grabbed the man's arm and shouted to Andy to help. They tumbled to the ground and overcame the man's physical resistance but couldn't get him to quiet down from causing such a scene. Mitch guided the man into the store and Andy carried the carton. They entered the front office. Normally, they would have gone to the back, but the man was creating too much of a scene. When someone persisted in banging on the door, Mitch investigated and discovered the man indeed had a wife in the store and through his investigative efforts determined the couple had attempted to pay for the logs but a cashier had made a mistake. Mr. Green had to be released and was offered apologies. It was not easy explaining to Andy how this bad stop had occurred, when he felt he had followed the basic rules of seeing the customer approach the goods, select them, had not paid for them, maintain an uninterrupted surveillance and stop the person outside the store. Thereafter, Mitch was no longer used to train new agents.

Analysis: *The agents assumed a man was engaged in an act of theft based on their adherence to fundamental principals of shoplifting detection: See the approach, the selection, taking of possession, concealment (if applicable), failure to pay, maintain an uninterrupted surveillance and stop outside. But there is another dimension to this business, which includes thinking through all other possible options, especially in a setting where goods are displayed beyond the registers. Even if they had known his wife was paying for merchandise and knew she had not paid for (or been charged for) the logs, some reasonable inquiry would have made sense. The agents could not have known if an arrangement had been made for the logs or not. In fact, the evidence clearly indicates the agents didn't even know he was a co-shopper and his wife was in the store at the counter purchasing merchandise. Numerous items of merchandise are displayed beyond the registers, and it's common practice to pay for the item before it's in the customer's possession. Once the man said his wife was paying or did pay for the item in question, it would have been prudent to wait until the wife arrived with the other purchases and examine the receipt. There's no harm in checking out a suspected customer's version of events if the story is at all* *plausible. If the man were lying about his wife coming shortly, that would surface soon enough. The customer's refusal and anger exacerbated the problem, but cooler security heads should prevail and never fuel an increasingly tense or potentially explosive situation. They moved too quickly.*

☯☯☯☯☯

Scenario 19A: (*Customer's Viewpoint*): It was such a nice morning, Sam felt like taking a walk and besides, he needed a pack of cigarettes. He knew he shouldn't be smoking, but a couple a day would do no harm. He left the senior citizen's apartments and strolled to the market just three blocks away. Upon entering the store, he noticed that one register was about to open, with no line, so he approached the cashier and said he wanted a pack of Vantage cigarettes. Cases of cigarettes were kept against the front wall of the market beyond the cashiers. Phil couldn't scan the item because it was still in the case, but he knew the price and keyed it into his terminal. Sam paid for the cigarettes, but didn't bother with a receipt because he had no bag. He walked over to the cigarette display cases, looking for his brand. The long rectangular doors that enclose the packs and the cartons of cigarettes were supposed to be kept locked, but they weren't. Sam lifted the Plexiglas door, removed a pack of Vantages and placed the pack into his shirt pocket. He then left the store to return to his apartment.

The man who approached and touched his arm startled him, and he jumped. Although having a hearing problem, he thought he heard the man say he wanted his cigarettes. Still startled, he thought the man was either a beggar or worse, and that he was about to be mugged or robbed. He started backing away, saying, "Get away from me, you bum, and leave me alone!" The younger man reached for him. Sam defended himself by trying to throw a punch; when he did that, he was quickly taken to the ground. Because he was a fragile and quite elderly man, the forcible contact with the parking lot surface broke two of his ribs, broke his glasses and cut his forehead, causing a stream of blood to flow down his face. He was assisted to his feet by the agent and another employee and returned through the store to the office in the rear. Inside the office Sam tried to explain he had paid for the cigarettes, but couldn't produce his receipt. Phil saw the agents bringing the old man back into the store and remembered Sam buying the cigarettes. As soon as he finished checking out a customer at the counter, he went to the back office, asked why his customer was in trouble. When told that the old gentleman had shoplifted cigarettes, he informed security that Sam had paid for the cigarettes and it was probably his fault for not getting the cigarettes for the customer or for not walking the customer over to the cases.

Scenario 19B: (*Employee's Viewpoint*) Manny had been in retail security for five years, had a good work record and was considered a good shoplifting operative. This day he was assigned to work the day shift at Store #78. Store #78 wasn't considered an exciting store to work, as not many arrests were made, so he figured it would probably be a slow day. He had just checked in with the Manager on Duty and before he could even get re-acquaint-ed with this store, observed an elderly gentleman walking along in front of the checkstands looking towards the cigarette cases. To Manny's absolute astonishment, the old man brazenly opened the cigarette case door (something customer's are not suppose to do), took out a pack of cigarettes, stuck them into his shirt pocket and walked out. Manny was right behind him, and caught the old man's attention by touching his arm and saying, "Sir! Sir! Excuse me, but I think you forgot to pay for your cigarettes. We need to talk about the cigarettes."

The old man jumped back, shouting, "Get away from me, you bum! These are my cigarettes!" Whoa, thought Manny, this is a feisty old goat who's been down this road before. He tried again. "Sir, I'm with store security. Give me those ciga-rettes." The customer started backing up and again, loudly told Manny to get away. Manny reached for the man's arm to stop his backward movement and the man swung his fist at Manny's face, missing by inches. That's it! said Manny to himself, as he seized the man's arm and forced him to the ground. The suspect hit his head on the pavement, started bleeding and complaining of pain in his chest. Another employee came out and helped Manny get the man up and into the store. The old man kept shouting, "Help! Help!" all the way in, causing everyone to stare at them. Once in the office he again asked for the cigarettes, but during the struggle apparently they had fallen out in the lot. The customer kept swearing at Manny and saying, "I paid for those damn cigarettes." About that time, Phil, one of the cashiers, stuck his head into the room and when told why they had the old man in custody, stated in fact that he had sold the elderly customer in custody the questioned cigarettes.

Analysis: *There was a local ordinance that required all stores to keep cigarettes under lock and key but this store failed to comply with that law. That law is aimed at keeping cigarettes away from children and teenagers. The agent seemingly acted in "good faith" and in keeping with the industry requirement of observing the customer approaching the case and selecting the merchandise. It never occurred to the agent the customer might have purchased the cigarettes first. In a strange way, the agent was a victim of circumstances just as much as the customer who ended up being victimized.*

The use of force, as evidenced by the serious injuries, was excessive; after all, this was an obvious senior citizen. Perhaps a younger man wouldn't have sustained such injuries. The cashier should have walked his customer to the merchandise to preclude the possibility of any misunderstanding and the cases should have been locked. Those failures contributed to what the agent believed was a theft committed in his presence. So it turns out that everything the store did was wrong.

Armed Security

Scenario #20: (*General Viewpoint*): An armed contract security guard was hired by a market chain to monitor the interior of the store and the doors. The agent observed a local shopper with a bulge in his jacket. The guard followed the customer outside and ordered him to stop. The customer panicked and ran. The guard chased the man across the lot, across the public street and into a residential neighborhood. He saw what appeared to be a carton of cigarettes being thrown onto the roof of a house. It was twilight and the streetlights had not yet come on. As the guard searched the backyard of one home, he pulled out his revolver. Suddenly he saw a figure loom up out of the dark. He reported that he thought the figure was coming at him, so he fired his gun at it. He had just killed the man who had attempted to steal a carton of cigarettes.

Analysis: *Professional security employees in the retail industry should have the kind of training that provides them with a realistic understanding as to the nature of this work, i.e., detecting people engaged in, more often than not, petty thievery. Most people who steal from retailers are neither dangerous nor hardened career criminals. That's not to say dangerous criminals don't engage in shoplifting, because they have and do. So approaching every suspected shoplifter with caution is only prudent. Just like state highway troopers who approach thousands of vehicle code violators in their career, the vast majority are only errant motorists. But the potential for running into a violent criminal is always there.*

In reality, most "shoplifters" aren't inherently "bad" people. They are moms, dads, husbands, wives, sisters, brothers, children, and friends, people who work for a living. About a quarter of them are teenage students. They sit around the family table at dinnertime, like we do. Their mistake is in succumbing to greed, succumbing to wanting something for nothing, who have a desire or compulsion to cheat and steal for a wide range of reasons which violate both God's and society's law. Many, if not most, are mortified when caught. And research indicates that only 1 in 20 resist.[3] If all the above is true, then why arm retail security? The bottom line is this: Retail security agents should be trained in understanding: 1) The above-expressed "ethics" of retail security; 2) the law that empowers them in their daily work; and 3) the legal concept of "the use of force." Some people, as a direct consequence of their conduct, may be injured during their pursuit, apprehension or arrest, and that's regrettable. But a person getting injured, let alone killed, is not security's intention.

---

3. *When Shoplifters Attack*, Security Management Magazine, June 1998

ꙮꙮꙮꙮꙮ

Security Do's and Don'ts

- **DO** summon medical assistance, if the person detained claims they are ill.
- **DO** provide the person detained with water, if they ask for it.

- **DO** allow a detained person the right to take their own medicine, if they so request.
- **DO** allow the person to use the phone, if there's an urgent need to do so, such as their child must be picked up at school.
- **DO** allow the person detained to use the restroom upon request.
- **DO** ensure the person is not too hot or too cold.
- **DO** ensure the person is not in discomfort (that is fixable).
- **DO** be courteous and professional in dealing with a person detained.
- **DO** check or cause to be checked a detained person's statement that someone is waiting for them inside or outside the store.
- **DON'T** threaten a detained person with any use of force, exposure or incarceration.
- **DON'T** make any promises of rewards, benefits or leniency in return for cooperation.
- **DON'T** use profanity, abusive, or offensive language at or in the presence of a person detained for shoplifting, even if provoked.
- **DON'T** belittle, make light of, laugh at or otherwise ridicule a detained person.
- **DON'T** eat in the presence of a detained person, unless you share with them. If you offer food, and the person declines your offer, then go and eat elsewhere.
- **DON'T** make any comments about a person's race, ethnic origin or religion.

The Grand Dilemma

Now that the reader has navigated this maze of definitions, explanations, descriptions, scenarios and do's and don'ts... it should be clear that this shoplifting phenomenon is indeed a grand dilemma. That dilemma is simply this: What are merchants to do? Should they let people carry away merchandise because of the many risks involved? Of course not! Never accuse anyone of stealing? Can't do that! Never chase or use force? That's the same as letting them carry away merchandise! What then are the options for retailers? They must have some detection capability. If thievery is such a problem, why don't the police or government provide protection?... because they couldn't possibly provide the necessary manpower required to deal with shoplifting, that's why. So merchants must hire their own protective force and deal with the inherent risks always connected with detection and apprehension, as discussed in this booklet.

The grand dilemma is also represented in the costs, all costs connected to shoplifting. Those costs include: Payroll for store security agents, television cameras, electronic detection equipment, article surveillance systems, mirrors, radios, insurance premiums, and workmen's compensation injury claims. Add to that the whopping $16 billion in stolen goods each year. And then add to that the costs of broken ribs, black eyes, deaths, jail time, humiliation, loss of jobs, rejection of employment applications (or subsequent termination for lying on an application for employment), denial of positions of trust or public office because of theft records, and on and on.... All this because of acts of thievery by millions of Americans and the merchant's need to survive by drawing a battle line. Talk about a "grand dilemma!"

About The Author

Charles A. Sennewald, CMC, CPP is an independent security management consultant and author of four books, _Effective Security Management, 3rd Ed._ 1998, _The Process of Investigation_, 1981, _Security Consulting, 2nd Ed._ 1996 and _Shoplifting_, (co-authored) 1992. Mr. Sennewald was the Director of Security for the Broadway Department Stores and was with that firm for 18 years. Prior to this he was Chief of Security for the Claremont Colleges and a Deputy Sheriff for the County of Los Angeles. Mr. Sennewald is the founder and first President of the International Association of Professional Security Consultants (IAPSC). He is a member of the American Society for Industrial Security and at one time was the chairman of the Standing Committee for Retail Security. He is a graduate of the California State University at Los Angeles, the L.A. County Sheriff's Academy and the U.S. Army's Military Police School. He commenced his consulting practice in 1979 and since then has serviced various national and local retailers in this country as well as Mexico. He has served, both for the plaintiff and the defense, as a consultant and expert witness in numerous law suits involving shoplifting incidents.